MIRIAM GREEN ELLIS

CHAMPION OF THE WEST

UNIVERSITY OF ALBERTA
LIBRARIES

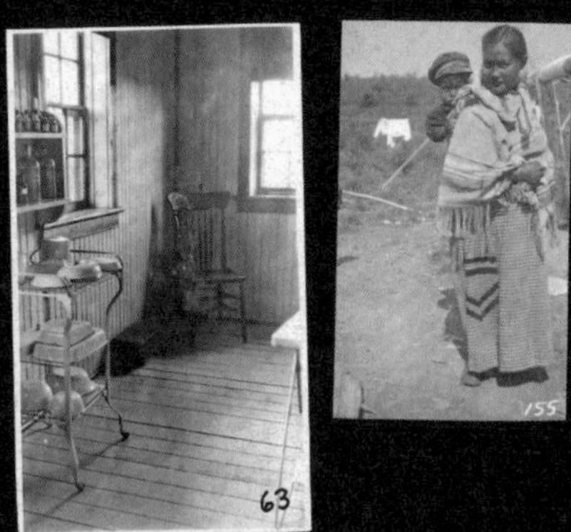

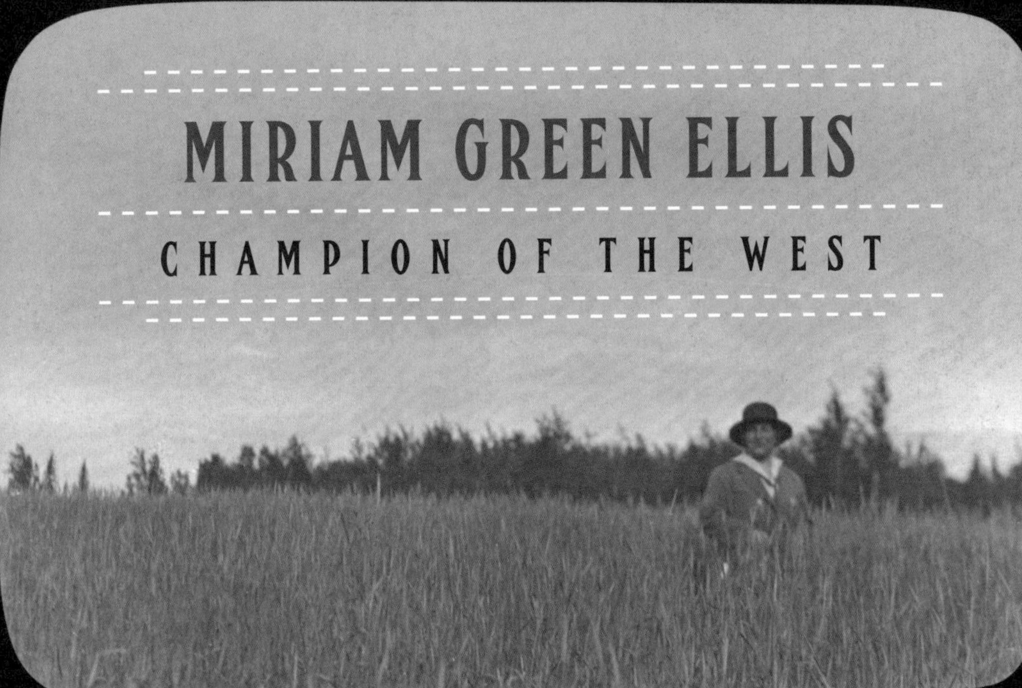

Patricia Demers

March 14 – May 31, 2013 Bruce Peel Special Collections Library University of Alberta

Locations and Destinations

From Athens to Aklavik and all across the West

Library and Archives Canada Cataloguing in Publication

Demers, Patricia
Miriam Green Ellis, champion of the West / Patricia Demers.

Includes bibliographical references.
ISBN 978–1–55195–315–1

1. Ellis, Miriam Green. 2. Agricultural journalists—Canada, Western—Biography. 3. Women journalists—Canada, Western—Biography. I. University of Alberta. Library II. Title.

PN4913.E55D46 2013 070.4'4963092 C2013–900298–7

Book design: Lara Minja, Lime Design Inc.
Editorial: Leslie Vermeer
Digital reproduction: Jeff Papineau
Exhibition installation: Carol Irwin
First edition, first printing, 2013

Printed in Canada

Canada
YUKON
Aklavik
Norman Wells
NORTHWEST TERRITORIES
NUNAVUT
Yellowknife
BRITISH COLUMBIA
ALBERTA
Fort McMurray
SASKATCHEWAN
MANITOBA
Edmonton
Prince Albert
Calgary
Saskatoon
Yorkton
Swift Current
Regina
Winnipeg
0 145 290 Miles
0 145 290 KM

Contents

Miriam's writing continues to offer a window on where we have come from.

Who Miriam Green Ellis Was and Was Not

MGE with camera: "Out west in the weekly" *The Slug* editorial supplement, *FHWS*, October 1951 96-91 MGE 11. IV

Left: MGE and Native woman and children, at Fort Resolution [magic lantern slide] 96-91 MGE S1

AN AGRICULTURAL REPORTER who cut her own path in the largely male-controlled field of journalism, Miriam Green Ellis (1879–1964) steered clear of the women's page and the society column. Though a lifetime member of the Canadian Women's Press Club from the beginning of her professional career, she was never grouped among the newsies, news hens, or paper dolls. Influences as well as innovations shaped her career. Aware of and indebted to the model of E. Cora Hind, crop forecaster *extraordinaire* for the *Winnipeg Free Press*, Ellis embraced broader agricultural fields. Beyond grain yields and her close knowledge of the maturing conditions of Canada's own Marquis wheat, MGE covered cattle show rings, bull sales, and stampedes, advances in vegetable, fruit, and seed farming, and Depression realities, even daring to address the topic of overproduction. As a traveller to the Northwest Territories, she knew she was stopping at many of the same places visited by Agnes Deans

MGE at Beaverlodge (undated) [photo album] 96-91 MGE 1.II

Cameron over a decade earlier. Yet the style and temperament of Cameron's *The New North* (1909) and Ellis's "Down North 1922" along with the dozens of newspaper articles she published on the trip to Aklavik are studies in contrast; so too are their respective magic lantern lectures. A strong advocate of women's right to vote and be considered persons, to drive cars, and to dress as they please, MGE delighted in shocking river steamer captains and livestock exhibit organizers by appearing in eminently practical breeches. A gifted raconteur, always moved by accounts of challenge and perseverance, she could poke fun at herself, rejoice and sympathize with others, and interject a tart observation when provoked. The fact that she bequeathed her papers to the University of Alberta is an invitation to uncover unique views of the West from an informed, widely travelled, passionate champion.

"A Good Scout"

THE MEMORY BOOK presented to Miriam Green Ellis in July 1940 by Winnipeg admirers describes the recipient as "everybody's friend" and "a good scout." At the time of Ellis's retirement in late 1952 from the *Family Herald and Weekly Star*, the Montreal-based newspaper billed as Canada's National Farm Magazine, for which she had served as Western Editor for 25 years, this scout registered satisfaction at "the very fine dinner, a wonderful turnout of some 100 colleagues, and dozens of telegrams and letters received," but also recorded some misgivings. Although she labelled the event "a big experience for a farm reporter," she ended the summary of festivities with the expressive, unelaborated twist

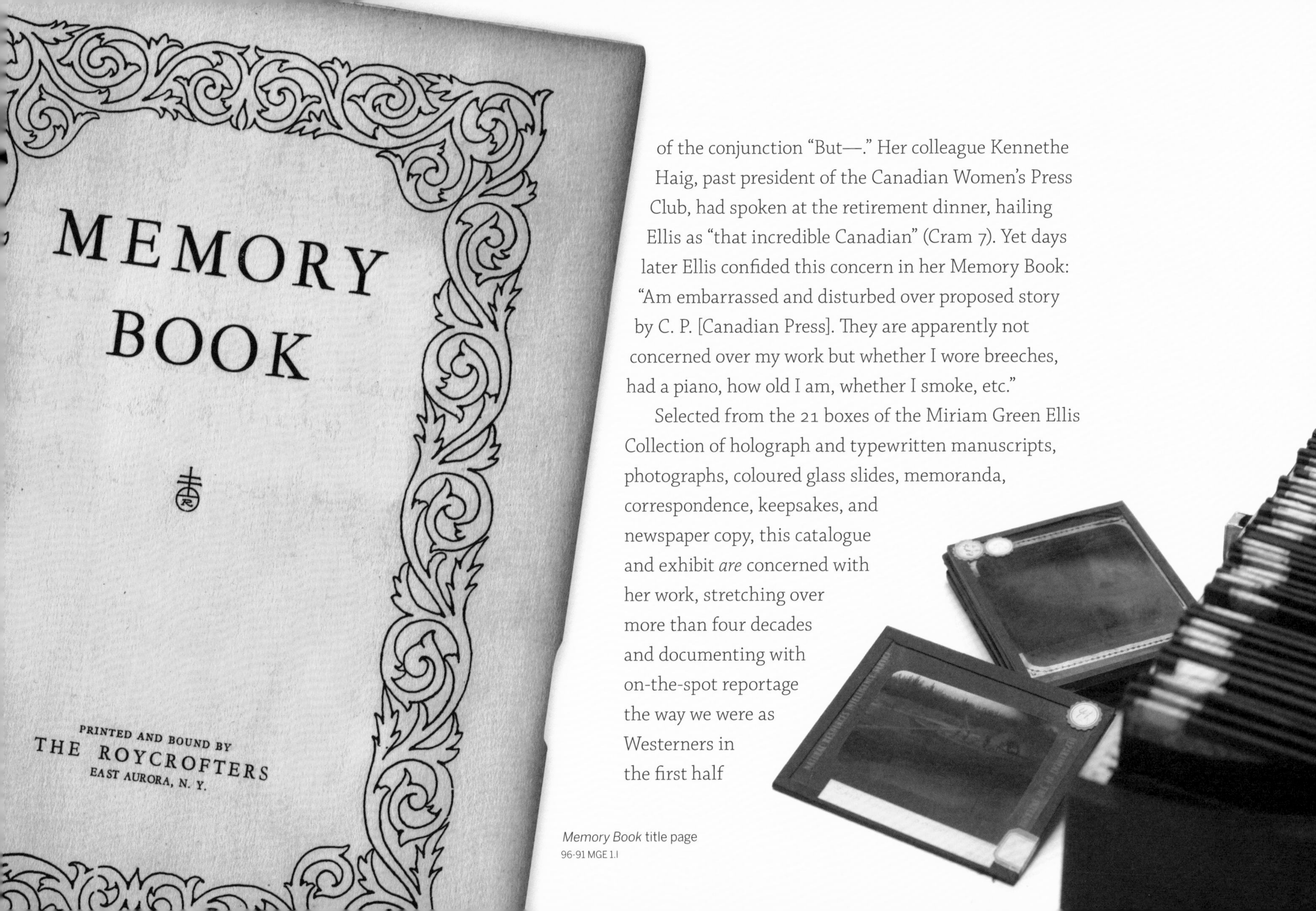

of the conjunction "But—." Her colleague Kennethe Haig, past president of the Canadian Women's Press Club, had spoken at the retirement dinner, hailing Ellis as "that incredible Canadian" (Cram 7). Yet days later Ellis confided this concern in her Memory Book: "Am embarrassed and disturbed over proposed story by C. P. [Canadian Press]. They are apparently not concerned over my work but whether I wore breeches, had a piano, how old I am, whether I smoke, etc."

Selected from the 21 boxes of the Miriam Green Ellis Collection of holograph and typewritten manuscripts, photographs, coloured glass slides, memoranda, correspondence, keepsakes, and newspaper copy, this catalogue and exhibit *are* concerned with her work, stretching over more than four decades and documenting with on-the-spot reportage the way we were as Westerners in the first half

Memory Book title page
96-91 MGE 1.1

Herald and Weekly Star, June 19, 1940

THE OLD GREY MARE, she ain't what she used to be." Neither are a lot of other things. I remember that old Buick car I was driving when war came on us in 1914. It was really in competition with the revered Model "T", but was too proud to admit it. The men around town said behind my back that I was a fool to think I could drive that car out to the lake —no woman could drive that road, they said.

Of course there were not many women driving in those days; like taking up the collection in church, it was really a man's job. No doubt it was rather a mean road; a trail, really, that wound in and out among the jack pines, and a foot deep in sand half the way. Those tires blown up to sixty or seventy pounds did not give very good traction in sand. If the road were a little uphill the tires just spun round and round, leaving a hole which complicated matters still more for the next car. I remember a couple such inclined bits of that lake road where half a dozen cars were regularly "grounded" any hot day. Spreading straw helped a little, or usually we just made a new trail through the jack pines and used that till the ruts got so deep it was as bad as the other.

We take today's cars for granted, but anyone who drove in those days will remember changing tires every few miles; we carried the extra tubes under the back seat together with a foot pump, and the tire was fastened to the wheel with three very firm steel rims. It was a major operation to remove those rims and another to put them back on; then more than likely the valve was leaking and it had to be done all over again. Everyone carried patches and a repair kiit with him. Spark plugs

Since before the last war the name of Miriam Green Ellis, western editor of The Family Herald and Weekly Star, has been familiar to farmers throughout Western Canada. Today, with the effects of total war hitting us on all sides, "MGE" philosophizes over some of the changes which have taken place since she first started to write of farms and farm homes of Western Canada.

Still hard at work as our readers can see every week, "MGE" is at present vice-president for Manitoba of the Canadian Women's Press Club as well as being associated with many other national and western organizations.

boys who could get a plane went barnstorming through the country. When the last war came we

rather than an invention of the Devil. No one had thought of standing up to it and beating it out with new varieties specially made for the purpose.

Milk wagons rattled through the streets fully equipped with dipper to ladle out milk into the customer's pail or jug. Today only a few who live beyond the end of the trolley know that milk of specified cream content does not grow in a bottle. Bread as well as bacon comes ready sliced.

In the last war there were mounted troops, but this time the hand is on the throttle rather than on the rein, and this is true on city streets as well as in the fields. The Marquis wheat went into the ground with the aid of a six-horse team, after the land had been thoroughly plowed and cultivated till the top was a nice, fine mulch. Today a one-way disk or similar implement drawn by a tractor speeds up and down the field to make a rough, cloddy surface. Since farm boys liked the smell of an engine exhaust better than manure, manufacturers built them more and better tractors. At first they were about as big as a threshing machine and just about as agile; then the pendulum swung back to a baby-buggy type. No sooner had they settled on a serviceable between-size model than along comes a baby Austin kind that "a lady can drive as well as a man, and that will stand without hitching." Its sponsors claim that it can do all the work done by a four-horse team, so it fits into the small farm and, like the Cadillac owner who keeps a Ford coupe for running around, large farm operators are buying the little tractor to do the chores around the garden and shelter belt.

As to frequent complaints that they tip over at the slightest provocation, the salesmen reply that if

the boys would slow down at the turns they would not upset. Any-

of the twentieth century. Contributing to a variety of newspapers—among them the *Prince Albert Daily Herald*, the *Regina Leader–Post*, the *Edmonton Bulletin*, and the *Vancouver Province*, as well as the *Family Herald and Weekly Star*—MGE criss-crossed Western Canada, relating stories of periods of boom, bust, and transformation. Hers was a strong personality, thoroughly engaged in the situation of the people and place she was covering—the furthest thing from remote, impersonal, dispassionate fact-finding. Even though MGE was, understandably, peeved at the preoccupation with sartorial fashion, it is worth observing that her immensely productive career also witnessed the passage from heel-hugging skirts to breeches and then tailored suits. MGE lives and is mirrored in her journalism; and so, while focusing on her writing, published and unpublished, this exhibit cannot decouple the writer and her words, but must also attend to the woman and spirit behind them.

"MGE looks back" *FHWS* 19 June 1940 96-91 11.1

A salient feature of MGE's writing is the ability to crystallize past and present, not without colourfully informed assessments. Assuming the role of an agricultural philosopher in "MGE Looks Back" (*FHWS*, 19 June 1940), she manages to avoid paeans to progress as well as nostalgic reminiscences. In the early stages of World War II, she chalks up the differences between then and now:

> Once again boys in khaki are on the streets, parading with their units, or in time off, walking with their girl friends. Twenty-five years ago, their mothers were making the momentous decision to marry before 'he' went over. But this time there are blue uniforms as well as khaki. There were airplanes in the last war, too, but at the end of the struggle aircraft were still so novel that returned boys who could get a plane went barnstorming through the country.

She also tabulates the changes in agricultural production attached to the two wars:

> When the last war came we had not realized there were such things as drought cycles; we did not know it was possible to grow too much wheat; we never dreamt the West would come to a time when it could actually boast of its dairy products and its fur farms. It was taken for granted that when the young men 'went West' they left the dairy cow behind, and that wild animals were hunted in the far North—not raised in coops. We did not think that Western prairies would ever need fertilizing. Somebody may have known about vitamins, but certainly it was not a word in the common vocabulary.

Top: Peace country farm [magic lantern slide]
96-91 MGE S1

Bottom: Wheat—Peace River [magic lantern slide]
96-91 MGE S1

Comparing the 1910s to the early '40s, she acknowledges that machinery for field and home now provides labour-saving efficiency:

MGE bookplate 96-91 MGE 2.X.5

> The Marquis wheat went into the ground with the aid of a six-horse team, after the land had been thoroughly ploughed and cultivated till the top was a nice fine mulch. Today a one-way disk or similar implement drawn by a tractor speeds up and down the field to make a rough cloddy surface. Since farm boys liked the smell of an engine exhaust better than manure, manufacturers built them more and better tractors.
> ... In the houses vacuum cleaners and washing machines have become standard equipment, and even in the country an electric refrigerator is not impossible. If the power line does not pass the door, a wind-charger stores electricity for lights, feed grinders, radio and all the rest.

The installation of radios on tractors, however, signals a more critical note: "In the old days philosophers and poets were made as thoughtful plowmen followed a trained team of horses up and down the furrows, but with the radio retailing 'swing' or war news, what chance has a man to think of the 'heavens and the earth, and all that in them is.'" The controlled, programmed mechanism of radio leaves her wanting more, since "there is no adventure of the unexpected." Toscanini sneaking in "an unrehearsed grace note or diminuendo" is likely "irritating to a radio producer." However, it is the natural cycle, with the effects of climate change as yet undetected, and quotidian worries that restore MGE's equilibrium: "Spite of all these differences, crocuses in fur jackets arrived in the spring of 1940 as they did in 1914; the wild geese winged North to their nesting; seed went into the ground; there is the same worry over acreages, prices, taxes, and tariffs. ... The essentials are the same, but the accessories are different."

Right: At Hay River [magic lantern slide] 96-91 MGE S1

“The essentials are the same,
but the accessories are different.”

A Conversationalist with a Sharp Eye, a Testy Tongue, and an Interest in People

A POPULAR SPEAKER. MGE fashioned her talks as informed, zesty conversations. When she addressed the triennial gathering of the Canadian Women's Press Club in Calgary in 1932, she suggested that "it is better for a special writer to be a reporter first and then develop along special lines" ("Special Fields"). Always in an engaging, face-to-face style, she admits

FAMILY HERALD AND WEEKLY STAR, WEDNESDAY, DECEMBER 18, 1929 THREE

WORLD'S BEST WHEAT FROM BUSH LAND

(Special Correspondence)

THE title of "world's wheat king" carries with it glamor enough, one would think, without the added glamor of romance which twice has given new lustre to the title.

Two years ago, the Peace River country of Alberta saw one of its young farmers, Herman Trelle of Wembley, win the title, thus showing to the world that the northern line for the growing of cereals was being pushed further north.

Then this year, with an exhibitor of the same name pushing him close, Joseph H. B. Smith of Wolf Creek, Alberta, is crowned wheat king of the world, while with his oats, he almost wins the double crown, taking second place with his Early Alaska variety, and fourth place with Victory, in another class.

And Wolf Creek, Alberta, is 120 miles west of Edmonton, ten miles north-east of the railway town of Edson on the Canadian National Railway.

It wasn't so many years ago, when, if a man said he was going homesteading in the Edson district, his friends sniffed pityingly at the "poor bush farmer," doomed for ever to a life of drudgery and an eternal battle against nature's heaviest odds.

Now, the Edson district houses a crown and its title, that of "world's wheat king," and a quiet, gentlemanly-looking farmer who homesteaded in that district from England, twenty-two years ago, has shown the world that even Alberta's so-called "bush land" can and does produce wheat that may be adjudged the best that can be grown anywhere.

Strange Coincidence.

If you happen to be fond of coincidences the fact that J. H. D. Smith of the Edson district had as his runner-up, C. Edson Smith of Montana, former title holder, should give you a thrill.

The wheat king was in Edmonton a day or two after the news of his success reached him over the long distance telephone from that city. He is tall, quiet, reserved—in bearing far from the type one would imagine as a "poor bush farmer". His black hair and well-trimmed, heavy moustache, and his upright and modest bearing, give him the touch of the military man.

"Did you expect to win the championship?" he was asked.

"Well, in a way I thought I might. I knew I had pure Reward wheat, and I knew it was good," he answered.

"How does it feel to be a world's champion?"

"Great! I had the feeling I was bound to win if I kept at it long enough," the wheat king replied.

And that apparently, is one of the secrets—perseverance, that old virtue we used to write in our copy books, but which, alas, few of us practice as we should.

"I've won over thirty grain prizes at the big Canadian and United States shows during the past thirteen years," Mr. Smith explained, "and I believed I could make the grade in time."

The winner of the title was born in Leicester, England, coming to western Canada in 1907, two years after Alberta

The major awards won at the International Live Stock show by Canadian exhibitors, were:

Grand championship wheat—Joseph H. B. Smith, Wolf Creek, Alta.; grand championship field peas—W. G. Gibson, Ladner, B.C.; reserve championship barley—Geo. Avery, Kelso; reserve championship peas—William Darnbrough, Laura.

Grand champion stallion, Clydesdale—James A. Johnstone, Yellow Grass; grand champion mare, Clydesdale—James A. Johnstone, Yellow Grass; junior champion stallion, Clydesdale—James A. Johnstone, Yellow Grass; senior champion mare, Clydesdale—James A. Johnstone, Yellow Grass; Scotland special Clydesdale team—James A. Johnstone, Yellow Grass.

Grand champion bull, Shorthorn—Fred Ont.; senior champion bull, Shorthorn—Fred H. Deacon, Unionville; H. Deacon, Unionville; junior champion bull, Shorthorn—T. A. Russell, Downsview, Ont.; grand champion female, Shorthorn—Fred H. Deacon, Unionville; senior champion female, Shorthorn—Fred H. Deacon, Unionville, Ont.; Shorthorn special bull award—Fred H. Deacon, Unionville, Ont.

Grand champion fat Lincoln wether—Robson and Goddard, Denfield, Ont.; grand champion ram, breeding Lincoln—Robson and Goddard, Denfield; grand champion ewe, breeding Lincoln—Robson and Goddard, Denfield; reserve grand champion ram, breeding Lincoln—Robson and Goddard, Denfield; reserve grand champion ewe, breeding Lincoln—Robson and Goddard, Denfield; grand championship carload lots, sheep—Robert McEwen, London, Ont.; grand champion, long wool type — Robson and Goddard, Denfield; reserve champion, long wool type—Robson and Goddard, Denfield; grand champion ram, breeding Oxfords—Russell Fleming, Whitby, Ont.; reserve champion ewe, breeding Oxfords—Russell Fleming, Whitby; reserve champion wether, fat Cotswold — Chas. J. Shore, Glanworth, Ont.; reserve champion ewe, breeding Cotswold—Chas. J. Shore, Glanworth; reesrve champion ram, breeding Cotswold—Chas. J. Shore, Glanworth.

JACK CANUCK RETURNS FROM CHICAGO

in her own case, "I did not deliberately choose agriculture as a special field. I drifted into it; having drifted, I like it." The impetus for this drift, she relates, was her trip by river steamer to Aklavik in 1922, where the zeal to collect stories had to be tempered with the responsibility of interpreting them.

> I was down the Mackenzie River a few years ago, and naturally I was not there just for my health. I wanted to get some stories, and the North is full of them. But approaching an old timer was difficult for patience and temper. After explaining what you wanted, the old timer was likely to look you up and down sceptically and infer, if he did not say, bluntly:
>
>> 'Now how do you think you are going to take a quick bolt into this country for a few days and then go away and write a story about it? If you could get old Captain Smith to write a story, you'd have a story.'
>
> Old Captain Smith is around eighty or ninety and likely can write his name but little else. So eventually you become rather belligerent, and ask them if they think Captain Smith will ever write a story. No, they don't suppose he will, but they are not inclined to think you will either. However, I feel a certain sympathy with them for their fear of being misinterpreted. But in the meantime, with the training of a reporter, and being brought up a Christian, I feel that I should be able to interpret them to the extent of my information.

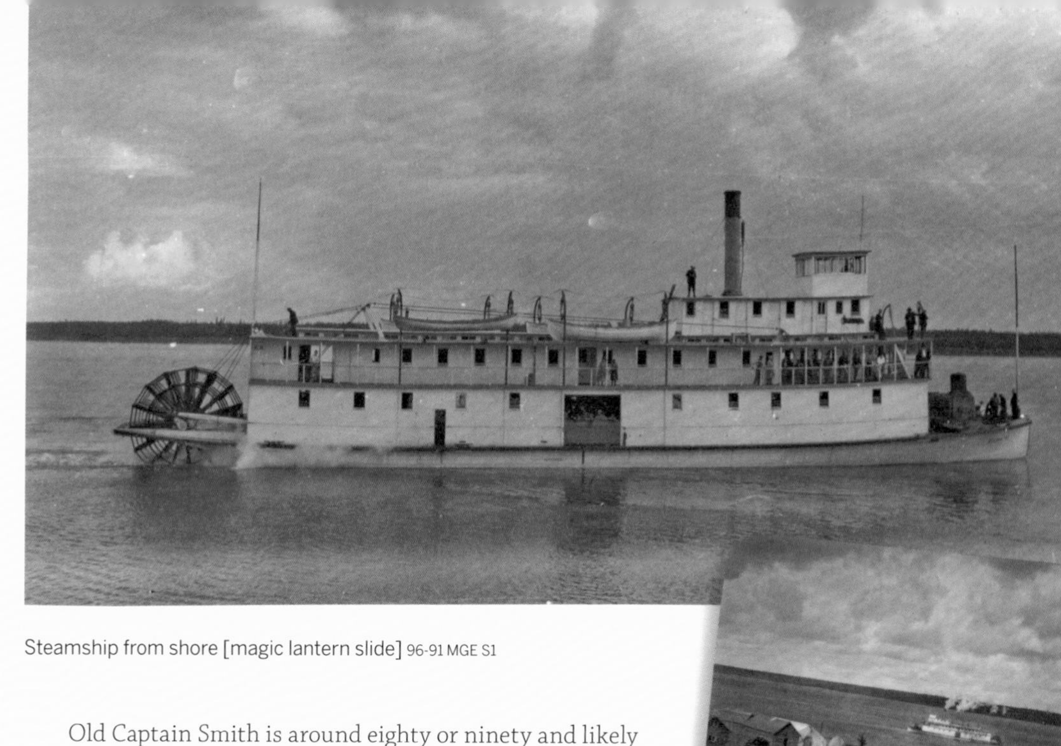

Steamship from shore [magic lantern slide] 96-91 MGE S1

Left: "World's Best Wheat from Bush Land"
FHWS 18 December 1929 96-91 MGE 8.1

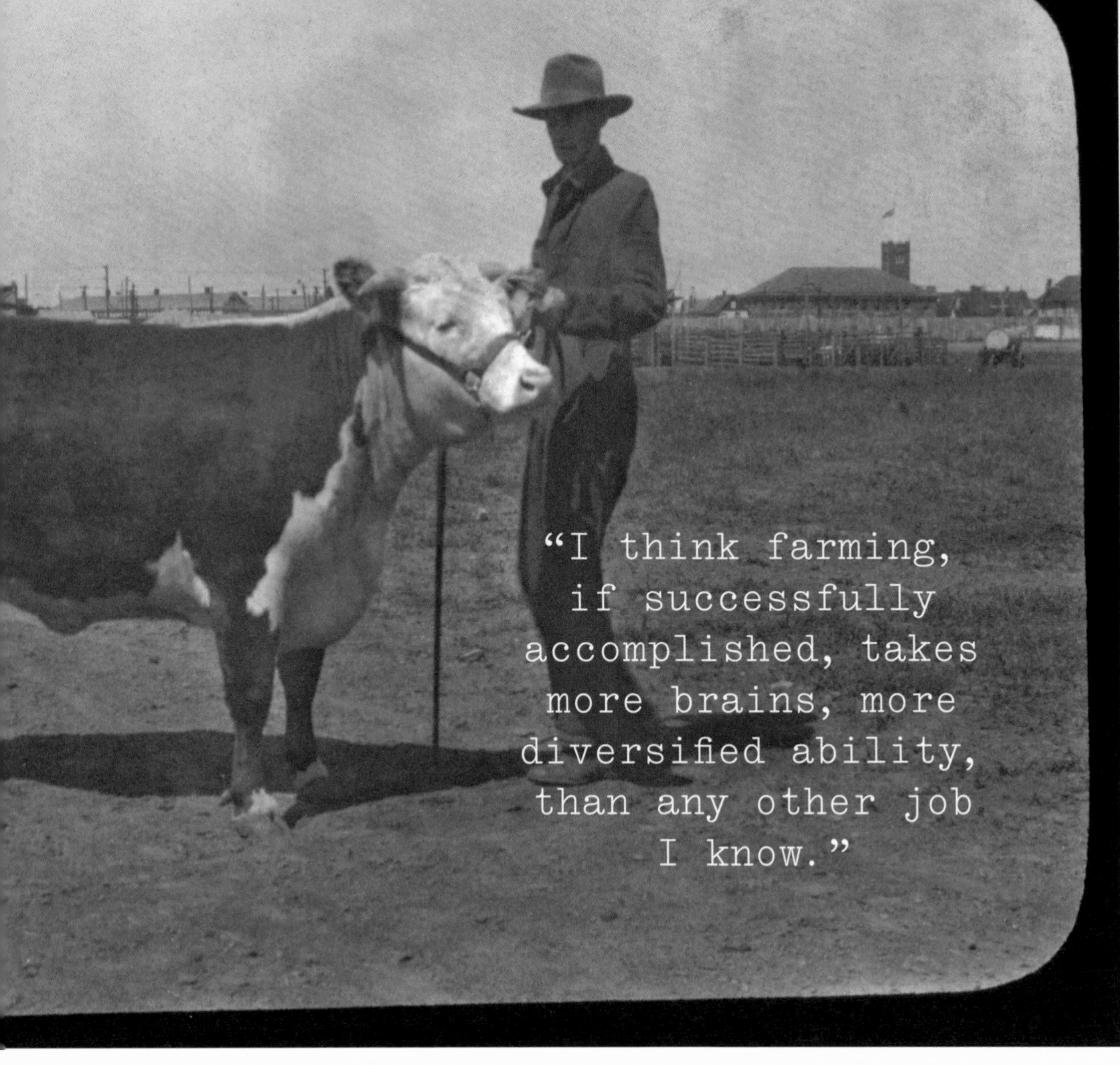

> "I think farming, if successfully accomplished, takes more brains, more diversified ability, than any other job I know."

Talking to the University Women's Club in Saskatoon in 1945, she underscored a claim her whole career illustrates: "I am interested in the agricultural end of this business all right, but I think I am even more interested in the people connected with this industry" ("Watching Other People Farm"). For this audience she pinned up her colours: "I think farming, if successfully accomplished, takes more brains, more diversified ability, than any other job I know." For the Rotary Ladies at Yorkton, MGE stressed the importance of detail and accuracy: "I am a reporter. I get what information I can and pass it on to the neighbours, the same as you do at the club, only I have to be more careful as to the accuracy of my statements for hundreds of thousands of people read it and believe it" ("Canada Has Something").

"Purebred Hereford Cow, Edmonton Exhibition" [magic lantern slide] 96-91 MGE S1

From Ontario to the West

WHO WAS THIS SELF-POSSESSED CHAMPION of the Canadian West and how did she come to look upon its thousands of farms—livestock, grain, fruit and vegetables, flowers and seeds—as her parish? Her back story is a series of arcs of discovery.

Miriam Green was born in Richville, New York, of Canadian parents, who returned to Canada and the paternal farmstead near Athens, Ontario, where this only child went to elementary school. Monitored by a double set of adult instructors, parents and grandparents, Miriam's childhood appears to have been exacting: the freedom of the farm also involved an obedient performance of chores and an acknowledgement of

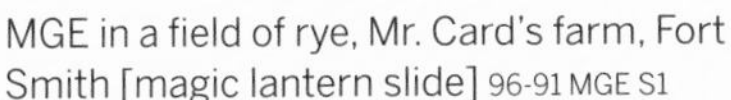

MGE in a field of rye, Mr. Card's farm, Fort Smith [magic lantern slide] 96-91 MGE S1

pioneer ingenuity. Speaking to the Manitoba Horticultural Association, MGE recalled the structures and smells, the rituals, and the chickens, turkeys, pigs, and mares of the eastern Ontario township home and farmyard.

> It was a square brick house built around 1860, when there was not much clearing around, either. There was a big living room which we called the Hall, and off it was a parlour where there was horsehair furniture and a piano, and off that again was the parlour bedroom. Grandfather's bedroom was on the other side of the Hall. Out behind the summer dining room were the summer kitchen and the pump, which had to be thawed out in winter, and then the ash house where we smoked our hams. It was behind the ash house that I buried my pet turkey when she died. Upstairs were bedrooms

Mrs. Thompson's garden, Bear Lake [photo album]
96-91 MGE 1.II

with dormer windows. Downstairs was a full-sized cellar that eventually housed a furnace. One room in the cellar was for apples, and what a nice smell that was. *That room was usually locked*. One room was for potatoes, not such a nice smell—and they had to be eternally picked over all winter; one room for wood for the furnace, and that was a gorgeous smell; there were shelves of fruit, a jar of yeast on the floor, crocks of eggs, and a pork barrel. My chief usefulness was in running errands up and down those cellar steps.

On winter nights we gathered round a cherry table and read. Grandfather had made that cherry table himself. There was a big kerosene lamp, and I was no sooner engrossed in *Bleak House*, or whatever I happened to be reading at the time, than I was sent down to the cellar for a dish of apples, and they had to be shined before they were brought in, too.

In that room was a long couch, the first piece of 'bought' furniture that grandfather and grandmother ever had. That was the room where we held our dances. In fact we hardly bothered to put down the carpet between dances. ("Western Homes I Have Seen")

Having "passed high-school entrance exams with honours before her tenth birthday" ("Miriam Green Ellis," *FHWS*, 17 December 1964), Miriam later attended Bishop Strachan School in Toronto and graduated from the Toronto Conservatory of Music with the A.T.C.M. (Associate of the Toronto Conservatory of Music). Her parents considered music-teaching a more suitable career for their daughter, who had wanted to pursue medicine.

The Green family's move to Edmonton in 1904 was followed by her marriage to George Edward Ellis, a graduate of Athens High School and Queen's University, in All Saints Anglican in June 1905. George Ellis was appointed by Minister of Education Alexander C. Rutherford as Inspector of Schools for the Province of Alberta in March 1906. These newlyweds (she was 26; he was 31) enjoyed some level of comfort and compatibility from the outset.

Discovery Well, Fort Norman [magic lantern slide] 96-91 MGE S1

Significance of Fort Norman

Fort Norman, **known today as Norman Wells, Northwest Territories, was Canada's first major oil discovery, with an oil-bearing formation discovered in 1911; from 1920 until 2004 it produced 226 million barrels. Imperial Oil built its refinery in 1937. Norman Wells provided an important source of oil for military manœuvres in Alaska and the Yukon during WW II.**

In addition to the shared background in small-town Ontario (Ellisville, George's birthplace, was a hamlet close to Athens), a retrospective picture of this marriage would disclose that they likely also agreed on many of the observations and recommendations in his annual reports about the state of schools in the Edmonton area. Although an admittedly indirect perspective on Miriam, about whose activities at the time little is known, the more available views of George indicate some of the possible topics of conversation for this couple. In 1906 he was recommending bonuses for teachers in outlying districts and suggesting that "the secret of success … lies in keeping these schools open the full year; otherwise the children soon forget what they have learned" (*Annual Report*, 1906, 53). He supported the building of "stables to accommodate the horses driven or ridden by the pupils," "bored wells" to provide good water, "the beautification of the school grounds or buildings," the provision of "a copy of the curriculum" for each teacher, and the holding

Prince Albert C1 Girls' Hockey Team, 1912
(photo courtesy Prince Albert Historical Museum)

of conventions "occasionally for a day, say, in the outlying parts of the inspectorate whence teachers seldom get to the central convention" (*Annual Report*, 1906, 54, 55). Inspector Ellis was especially concerned about teaching based on and reflecting surrounding conditions, lamenting that "many teachers [of Nature Study] are always wanting to teach a book instead of nature itself" (*Annual Report*, 1906, 54). However, he reserved the least pessimistic forecast for "the establishment of a University in the near future," as a result of which "there will be no need for anyone to hesitate coming to this country, for we will then have all the educational facilities that even a connoisseur could wish for, as well as a land teeming with wealth for the agriculturalist and the manufacturer" (*Annual Report*, 1906, 55). Ellis resigned his position in 1909 to pursue graduate work, accompanied by Miriam, likely in Chicago.

The next appearance of Miriam in any archive is her role in Prince Albert, Saskatchewan. In 1912 she started and managed the girls' hockey team of the Prince Albert Collegiate Institute, where George was principal. Based on reports in the *Prince Albert Daily Herald*, Miriam acquired a considerable reputation as a curler. While living in Prince Albert, she signed on formally in 1913 as a member of the Canadian Women's Press Club, which, making history as well as news,

Edmonton Women's Press Club 1913, MGE far right [photo album] 96-91 MGE 1.II

boasts "the longest continuous existence of any professional women journalists' organization in the world" (Jackel 53). MGE renewed her affiliation as an active member until her death in 1964. She also began writing for the local paper, though the lack of bylines makes her contributions impossible to identify. Equally difficult to trace is the fault line in the childless marriage.

The outbreak of war in August 1914 affected the status of this couple, as it did for millions of others. It drew attention to the importance of the field that was to become Miriam's livelihood and the suffragist principles that propelled farm organizations. With grain and livestock production of key importance, the war "greatly enhanced the value of the Canadian grain belt in international economy" (Wood 290), prompting generous responses in manpower and farm yields from the West. While "for the most part uncomplainingly" accepting conscription, Manitoba grain

MGE at "Limberlost," north of Prince Albert, Saskatchewan [photo album]
96-91 MGE 1.1

growers pledged the returns of one acre of grain "to the needs of the Empire": the Saskatchewan Co-operative Elevator Company agreed to mill a "patriotic acre," and the Alberta Grain Growers contributed products and money, "twelve thousand dollars to various funds in 1916" (Wood 290–91). War conditions also hastened the arrival of the enfranchisement of women, granted in all three provinces in 1916 and fuelled largely by the initiatives of farm women. Separate organizations of farm women were formed first in Saskatchewan in 1914, followed by the United Farm Women of Alberta in 1915 and the Manitoba Farm Women in 1916, all supporting public health and education in rural communities, the need for obstetrical nurses, and the temperance cause. The war "changed the status of women in journalism," too, bringing them new opportunities and professional responsibilities ushering in "an era in which the CWPC's power and prestige steadily advanced" (Oliver 12).

On February 18, 1915, George enlisted as a major in the 53rd Battalion of the Canadian Expeditionary Force; his Attestation Paper lists Miriam as his wife. According to his personnel record, he was "dismissed" and returned to eastern Ontario, to the Leeds County area of his birth. From 1922 until 1938 he taught mathematics and geography at Lisgar Collegiate Institute in Ottawa. Meanwhile Miriam, who always published under the name Miriam Green Ellis, lived in Edmonton and, later, Winnipeg. No record of a divorce exists.

Her career as cub reporter in Prince Albert and Regina moved to its next stage when she secured a position as a staffer at Frank Oliver's *Edmonton Bulletin,* covering the legislature as well as cattle shows and small-town fairs. Here was an independent woman making her own way in a male-dominated field. Her lifelong commitment to the Canadian Women's Press Club reveals remarkable professional and personal loyalties, connecting her to the

"Bull sale, 1920" [photo album]
96-91 MGE 1.II

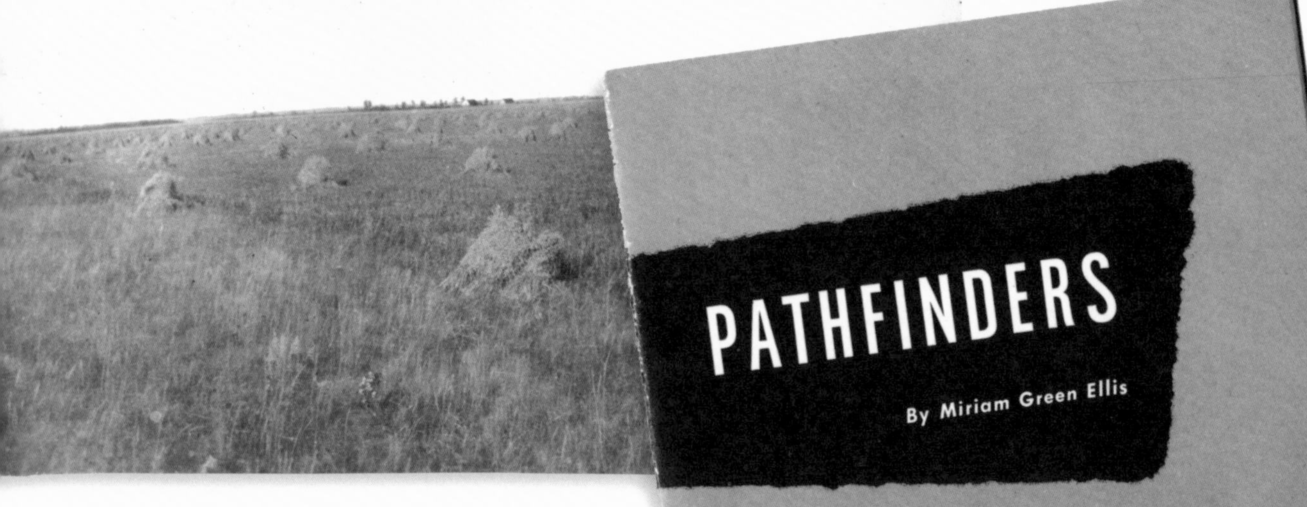

tradition of Kathleen 'Kit' Coleman, co-founder and first president of the CWPC; Nellie L. McClung, suffragist, social activist, politician, and fiction writer; Violet McNaughton, founder of the Saskatchewan Women Grain Growers; and E. Cora Hind, whom she succeeded as Western Canada's premier agricultural journalist. Her tribute to these forerunners and contemporaries, delivered as a talk, *Pathfinders*, at the 1956 CWPC Triennial in Edmonton, indicates the breadth of this network of press women and MGE's zest and sense of belonging.

Miriam's year as Edmonton president of the CWPC, 1919, characterized not only by her preparation of "Bohemian refreshments" for the "soiree[s]" ("John Hunt is Honor Guest," n. pag.) but also by an engagement with a larger community, was certainly covered in the *Bulletin*. Speakers and invited guests for the year included Father Drummond of the Jesuit College; legendary Winnipeg press woman E. Cora Hind, whom Ellis introduced as "being called on to do the work of three men for half a man's salary" ("Press Club Entertains," n. pag); University of Alberta Dean of Agriculture E.A. Howes and Acting President William Kerr; aesthetic dancer Ruth St. Denis; Premier Charles Stewart; and mountaineer Mary Jobe.

Above left: Spirit River Oats [photo album] 96-91 MGE 1.II
Above right: *Pathfinders* 96-91 MGE 2.X.12

Facing page: Map of MGE's journey (courtesy University of Alberta Press)

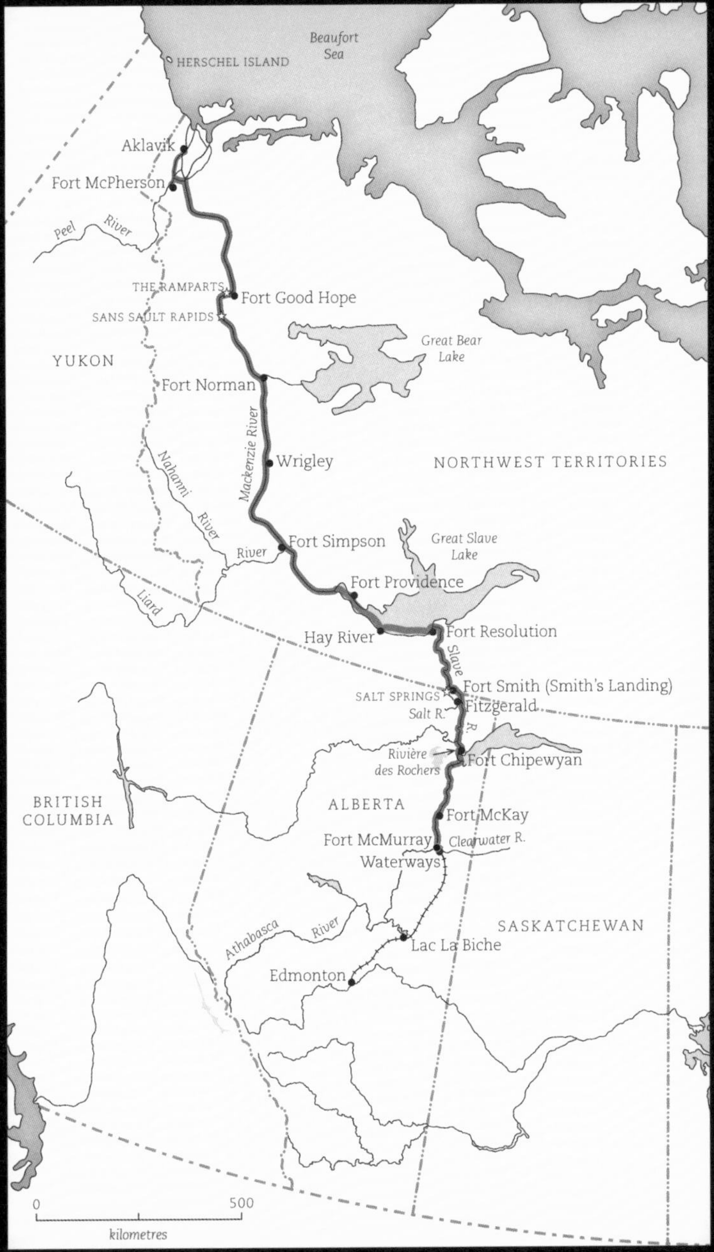

Journey to Aklavik, NWT

THIS MAJOR ADVENTURE in the summer of 1922 was a turning point in MGE's career. Having failed to convince editor Frank Oliver of readers' interest in reports of such a trip, with typical self-possession and entrepreneurial aplomb, she granted herself a leave of absence from the *Bulletin*. In mid-June, she departed from the Edmonton train station, having been wished farewell by Nellie McClung, who presented her with a bouquet of flowering sweet peas. Stopping at Lac La Biche en route to Waterways, the terminus of the Alberta and Great Waterways Railway, south of Fort McMurray, MGE proceeded by river steamer down the Athabasca to Fort Chipewyan and Fitzgerald. After 'portaging' to Fort

Above: Going up the Clearwater River [magic lantern slide] 96-91 MGE S1; cook, "Doc" Griffin, with lake trout caught near Great Slave Lake [magic lantern slide] MGE S1; mother and child with caribou skin hood and coat [magic lantern slide] MGE S1

She prepared an album of 237 black-and-white photographs, over half of which she had transferred to coloured glass slides.

New Steamer Service

Season 1923

A & A TRANSPORTATION COMPANY LIMITED

Season 1923

Alberta & Arctic Transportation Company Limited

10056 100th St., Edmonton, Alta.

Operating from WATERWAYS, ALBERTA (The Terminus of The Alberta and Great Waterways Railway Company), To the Arctic Ocean and Points on the Athabasca, Slave, Mackenzie, Liard, Nelson, Peel and Great Bear Rivers and Athabasca and Great Slave Lakes

The Midnight Sun—Mackenzie River Delta

Steamship "Distributor" on Mackenzie River

Passengers will leave Edmonton on the 12th of June and connect with the Steamer "Distributor" at Fort Smith on her long trip to the Arctic. The return trip from Edmonton will occupy about one month's time. The company will sell a special round trip ticket from Waterways, the terminus of the Alberta and Great Waterways Railway, to Aklavik, at the mouth of the Mackenzie River, for $240.00, a total mileage of 3,332 miles. Meals and berths are not included in the price of this ticket and will have to be paid for at regular rates.

The "Lady Mackworth," which pushes a covered barge, ...uipped with sleeping and dining room accommodations, starting ...out June 1st, will operate between Fort Smith and ...olution on Great Slave Lake. As soon as it is ascertained Great Slave Lake is clear of ice this Gasboat will proceed ...e on the north arm of the lake. From Rae she will pro... ...ia Resolution on her

Liard River Service

...Simpson about July 2nd, for Liard. On her return ...n about the 7th, she will again ascend the Liard and ...vers to Nelson. On her return to Simpson from ... will be available for any work on the navigable ... of Fort Smith, including Great Bear River

...ouse Boat on Great Slave Lake

Passenger Rates

(Meals and berths are not included in Passenger R...

ATHABASCA, SLAVE AND MACKENZIE R... SERVICE

Mileage	From Waterways to—	Downstream from Waterways
6	McMurray	$ 1.00
40	McKay	5.00
153	Pt. Brule	9.50
176	Lake Athabasca	13.50
192	Chipewyan	15.00
222	Mouth of Peace River	18.00
292	Fitzgerald	22.00
308	Fort Smith	27.00
352	King's Sawmill	31.50
512	Resolution	37.00
587	Hay River	42.00
621	Wrigley Harbor	45.00
665	Providence	47.00
821	Simpson	57.00
973	Wrigley	67.00
1,125	Norman	77.00
1,175	Norman Oil Well (Discovery)	82.00
1,298	Good Hope	87.00
1,512	Arctic Red River	97.00
1,566	McPherson	102.00
1,666	Aklavik	107.00

LIARD RIVER SERVICE

	From Simpson to—	Upstream from Simpson	Downstream from Nelson
120	Mouth of Nahanni River	$15.00	$40.00
215	Liard	25.00	30.00
390	Nelson	50.00	20.00

From Simpson to Liard round trip occupies about 5 days.
From Simpson to Nelson round trip occupies about 10 days.

MEALS ON STEAMERS AND GASBOATS

Breakfasts ... $ .75
Dinners and Suppers ... 1.00

BERTHS ON STEAMERS

Lowers, per night ... $1.50
Uppers, per night ... 1.00

SMITH PORTAGE SERVICE

Fitzgerald to Fort Smith (either way) ... $5.00

Tickets sold at above rates are good for continuous passage only. The company reserves the right to refund any portion of fare to any landing shown in the tariff where, in the opinion of the master, it is unsafe to land. All tickets issued for passage on the Steamers and Gasboats of the Company are sold subject to the contract endorsed on ticket.

Children over five years of age and under twelve years will be charged half fare.

Passengers landing at points not shown in this tariff will be charged a proportionate rate according to mileage.

BAGGAGE

One hundred and fifty pounds of personal baggage will be carried free with each full fare, and seventy-five pounds with each half fare on Steamers only. Freight rates will be charged on all baggage across Smith Portage. Personal baggage carried entirely at passenger's risk.

Smith (Smith's Landing) in a Winston auto, she boarded a larger river steamer for the trip down the Mackenzie, with stops at Fort Resolution, Hay River, Fort Providence, Fort Simpson, Fort Norman (Norman Wells), Fort Good Hope, Fort McPherson, and finally Aklavik.

MGE did not travel alone; she was one of at least fourteen passengers, including an uncle and aunt from Pennsylvania, John and Ethel Carley (who may have shared some of the fare). Although in "Down North" Miriam vowed to keep "a regular diary of this trip," she actually produced three distinct texts: the promised diary, 249 small pages (3.5" x 6") of mainly typed daily diary entries, which are really shorthand notes to self, an index of names, and demographic information relating to the 1922 journey; the typescript travelogue "Down North" (published for the first time, along with samples

Left: Steamship "Distributor" [magic lantern slide] 96-91 MGE S1

Right: Promotional brochure for Alberta and Arctic Transportation Company Ltd., 1923 96-91 MGE 3.IV

Facing page: "Eskimo's first ride in automobile" [magic lantern slide and photo album] 96-91 MGE S1 and 1.II

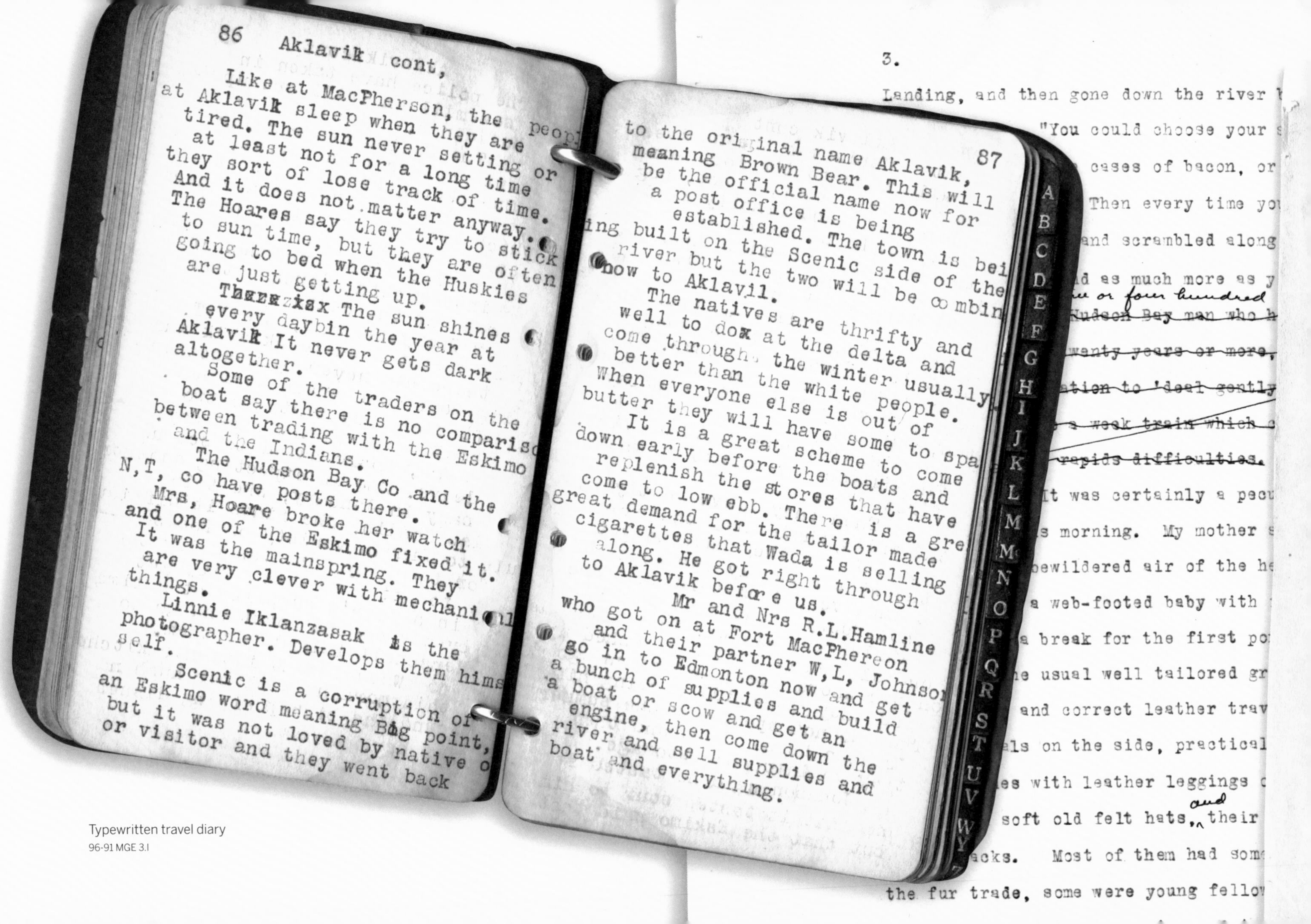

86 Aklavik cont,

Like at MacPherson, the peopl
at Aklavik sleep when they are
tired. The sun never setting or
at least not for a long time
they sort of lose track of time.
And it does not matter anyway.
The Hoares say they try to stick
to sun time, but they are often
going to bed when the Huskies
are just getting up.
Thezzzxzx The sun shines
every daybin the year at
Aklavik It never gets dark
altogether.
Some of the traders on the
boat say there is no compariso
between trading with the Eskimo
and the Indians.
The Hudson Bay Co and the
N,T, co have posts there.
Mrs, Hoare broke her watch
and one of the Eskimo fixed it.
It was the mainspring. They
are very clever with mechani[cal]
things.
Linnie Iklanzasak is the
photographer. Develops them hims[elf]
self.
Scenic is a corruption of
an Eskimo word meaning Big point,
but it was not loved by native o[r]
or visitor and they went back

to the original name Aklavik, 87
meaning Brown Bear. This will
be the official name now for
a post office is being
established. The town is bei[ng]
ing built on the Scenic side of the
river but the two will be combin[ed]
now to Aklavil.
The natives are thrifty and
well to dox at the delta and
come through the winter usually
better than the white people.
When everyone else is out of
butter they will have some to spa[re]
It is a great scheme to come
down early before the boats and
replenish the stores that have
come to low ebb. There is a gre[at]
great demand for the tailor made
cigarettes that Wada is selling
along. He got right through
to Aklavik before us.
Mr and Nrs R.L.Hamline
who got on at Fort MacPhereon
and their partner W,L, Johnson
go in to Edmonton now and get
a bunch of supplies and build
a boat or scow and get an
engine, then come down the
river and sell supplies and
boat and everything.

3.

Landing, and then gone down the river
"You could choose your
cases of bacon, or
Then every time you
and scrambled along
d as much more as y
~~Hudson Bay man who h~~
~~wenty years or more,~~
~~ation to 'deal gently~~
~~a week train which~~
~~rapids difficulties.~~
It was certainly a pecu
s morning. My mother
bewildered air of the h
a web-footed baby with
a break for the first po
he usual well tailored gr
and correct leather trav
als on the side, practical
es with leather leggings
soft old felt hats, and their
acks. Most of them had som
the fur trade, some were young fellow

Typewritten travel diary

96-91 MGE 3.1

of her fiction, in *Travels and Tales of Miriam Green Ellis: Pioneer Journalist of the Canadian West*, University of Alberta Press, 2013); and a series of more than forty newspaper articles based on segments of the trip. She also prepared an album of 237 black-and-white photographs, over half of which she had transferred to coloured glass slides to illustrate her subsequent magic lantern lecture, "The Land of the Midnight Sun," delivered across the country and in New York state. She even drafted a radio play, *Their Northern Exposure*, incorporating stories from the Aklavik trip as related by northern bush pilots. Two of her unpublished short

ANNOUNCING

Miriam Green Ellis
IN A LECTURE
ON HER
UNIQUE TRIP TO
The Land *of the* Midnight Sun

CANADA'S NORTHLAND, with its mysterious lure, its wonderful scenery and its potential resources, is the last of the unknown lands. The lecturer takes her audience down the MacKenzie River to the very delta where it empties itself into the Arctic Ocean Along the route one sees the various tribes of Indians and last of all the Eskimo, who live in and around the MacKenzie Delta.

MRS. ELLIS is a well-known newspaper woman of Edmonton, Alberta, and so was naturally adapted to catch the features of the trip, which she took last year. As vice-president of the Canadian Women's Press Club, she became well known to the women of her craft throughout Canada, and her stories of the North have appeared in newspapers across the Dominion, and in various magazines, English and American.

Nearly one hundred beautiful slides illustrate this unusual story of far away lands and people.

This page: Promotional material for "Land of the Midnight Sun" lecture
96-91 MGE 1.IV

MIRIAM GREEN ELLIS
10044 107TH STREET
EDMONTON
ALBERTA

Down North 1922

Since I was a small girl in pinafores and was taught that
he earth was round and flattened a little at each end like an
pple, I have wanted to go to the place where it started to
latten. It seemed to me that if one were careful not to slip off
he edge, one could probably see the pole in the distance and
lso see if the firmament wrapped itself around the earth
r if it were jus
orning , as I sat
urls to dry, I ha
arth really did r
eally were round,
id not drop off; w
ent at night and w
Years pa
ntricate problems;
adio and the Book c
uggested to my edit

TORONTO TELEGRAM November 28, 1923

Magic Journey North
To Land of Midnight Sun

Miriam Green Ellis Gives Fascinating Illustrated Lecture to University Women

Not in months has a Toronto woman's club provided such a fairy tale evening as that of the University Women's Club last night. Into the charming madonna blue and grey hall of the Women's Union, St. George Street, their audience entered. Dark went the lights, and for almost two hours they sat entranced as they took a magic journey to Canada's Land of the Midnight Sun.

Tap went the long cane of Mrs. Miriam Green Ellis, of Edmonton, and scene after scene of the path- ... Midnight Sun

and its branches, and to see the primitive beginnings of the new settlements along its way was like turning the pages of Canada's history back three hundred years. Past wildernesses of fine trees and glimpses of picturesque water falls, over river rapids, her audience went. Mrs. Ellis had not been satisfied merely to stay on her boat. When it paused to load freight or because of unfavorable weather conditions—when on the Great Slave Lake for instance—the boat does not proceed when it is rough—Mrs. Ellis took inland jour-

Left: "Down North" [typescript]
96-91 MGE 3.II

"Alone" [typescript] 96-91 MGE 2.III
"A War Bride's Return" [typescript] 96-91 MGE 2.IV

Miriam Green Ellis

A War bride's Return

John ~~Bear~~ McDougall was on the way to the station to meet his fair haired bride, whom he had left in England, the day of their marriage seven months before, It was still an hour before the train was due, and as he walked Westward, along the broad Edmonton street, his steps were slow, his eyes thoughtful. He saw none of the crowds that jostled him on their way to the theatre, saw none of the beauty of that glorious summer evening. Although he was looking right at it, he did not realize the beautiful sun-set with its brilliant, but soft blending colors of rose and purple. Ordinarily John Bear loved those sunsets, that seem more brilliant in Western Canada, than anywhere else and many a time he had tried to describe them to ~~Rose~~ Margaret, who could not believe that in June, the nights never got really dark; ~~it did not really get dark at all;~~ that the city lights were not put on till close to eleven, and that there was a reflection of the sunset in the sky all ... look of surprise that came

6,500 Words

MIRIAM GREEN ELLIS
10044 107TH STREET
EDMONTON
ALBERTA

"Alone."

A footfall - every nerve in John Carson's body
... into knots; but it was only a rabbit thumping
the woods.
He cursed himself for a fool and a coward.
... ingrowing and unceasing, gripped him in its
...ke the devilfish, its victim. As time passed,
...hes grew stronger and stronger, till he wondered
... longer he could withstand the vicious monster.
"Oh, God," he said wearily, as though it were
...ny times rehearsed, "why did I bolt like a
...? Anythi... ...ld have been better than this
...kulking."
Carson s...
...he had ...
...ntly s...
... the I...
...e wate...
...d whi...
... to th...
Indians. They believed ...
...pirit, who came to this restless steaming pool at

" Alone,""
Written by Miriam Green Ellis from a true incident
Return postage enclosed, 6¢

Original Version

stories, also likely germinated in the trip North, focus on Native–White relations in surprising and unsettling ways. "Alone" explores the sympathetic bond between a hunted White man and the Native girl he abducts, while "A War Bride's Return" creates a fraught contact zone exposing hypocrisy and racism when a sheltered English girl enters a Native settlement north of Edmonton. Together they not only testify to MGE's purposiveness, curiosity, and determination, but afford an unparalleled, ethnographic portrait of the Great Northwest.

MGE writes candidly about the process and pitfalls of composition en route. Uncle John handily devised "a typewriter table that is as neat as a pocket in a shirt—just the very thing," while Aunt Ethel proofread Miriam's "Eskimo stories" (Diary, 22, 121). As a diarist and a traveller meeting different adventures each day, MGE faced the time-consuming task of converting her diary entries into fuller notes. On July 15 she conceded: "worked on my notes for some time during the day. Wish I had done them as I was going along, instead of writing them in diary form, but I did not know till I had them what I wanted to write about" (Diary, 121). On eventful days she had to work at "trying to get up the courage to start some writing" (23 July, 165). A few personal connections do not find their way into "Down North"; only in the diary do we discover that Mrs. McClung sent her a telegram on the second day (7), that "the sweet peas Nellie brought to the station" (8) are still doing nicely in the coffee can, and that "Wop" (WW I flying ace Wilfrid Reid) May met her "at the station" on her return (174).

Wop May [photo album]
96-91 MGE 1.II

Advert for May Airplanes from *Edmonton Bulletin* 4 March 1920 96-91 MGE 21.V

Kindred Spirits

Taken at the Lacombe airfield, **south of Edmonton, these photos, with Miriam's own quasi-ferocious Gaelic notation "Wha daur meddle wi' me," illustrate her close friendships with WW I flying ace "Wop" (Wilfrid Reid) May and writer Nellie McClung, who clearly enjoyed her company and zest.**

When we aviate 1920

NELLIE L.

Florence MGE Wop & Tubbie

"Wha daur meddle wi' me"

NELLIE L

Above: Wop May [photo album] 96-91 MGE 1.1
Below: "When We Aviate" [photo album] 96-91 MGE 1.1

Her journey from the metropole to the periphery, to borrow Mary Louise Pratt's terminology, is actually very attentive to "the reverse dynamic" (Pratt 4), that is, to the power of the rural conveyed back to the urban. In "Down North" Ellis emerges for me not as "the 'seeing [wo]man,'" Pratt's "admittedly unfriendly label for the white ... subject ... whose imperial eyes passively look out and possess" (9), but rather as an engaged, curious citizen who enacts the drama of departure and return without overlooking experiences of frustration and disjunction.

"Down North" is full of vivid portraits, textual and photographic, of fellow passengers. With a hint of disbelief she describes Gladys Patterson, "a girl from Yorkshire, England, going down to marry a chap at Norman" whom "she has not seen ... since the war and of course has not heard from him since last Fall some time, but she does not seem to have any doubts in the matter." At the Edmonton train station she meets Bishop Grouard, the Oblate missionary who oversaw the immense vicariate of Athabasca–

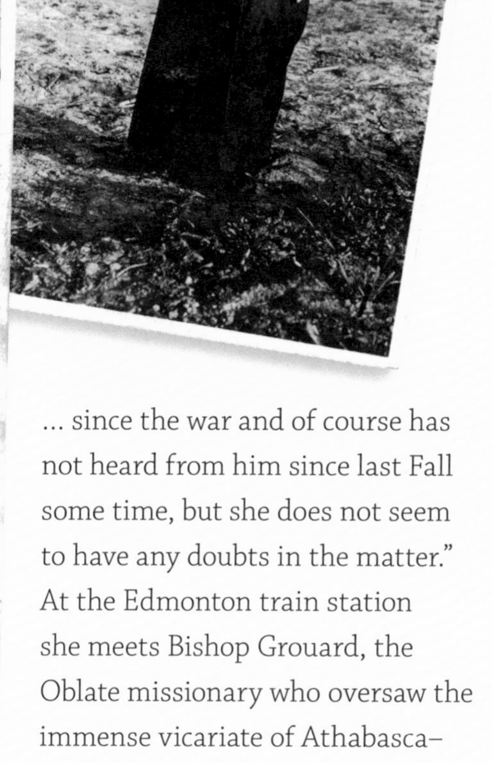

Left: "Miss Patterson at Lac La Biche" [photo album] 96-91 MGE 1.III

Right: Bishop Émile Grouard at Edmonton train station [photo album] 96-91 MGE 1.III

Mackenzie and brought the first printing press to Athabasca country: "He has been in the north for half a century and knows every white man and Indian right down to the Arctic. ... He is well over eighty now but still carries on as active head of his big diocese." Although not photographed, botany professor Roland Holroyd from Pennsylvania State University is initially an instructive source—"it will be interesting getting some first-hand information about the plants and flowers"—but soon proves a disappointment when he refuses or is unable to identify any vegetation. Her frustration with this reclusive passenger is evident when she comments on his attempted moustache, "a rather anaemic affair."

> After weeks of sober living he has suddenly given way to smoking cigarettes, but he does it very genteelly, using a six-inch amber holder. We have warned him to be careful, as dear knows what would grow there if the wooly down were burned off. Poplar comes where spruce has been burned off, we tell him; maybe feather follows down.

When her sympathies are engaged, MGE's writing can convey an awareness of ethical dilemmas and well-cultivated advocacy. At Fort McPherson, the young prisoner Alikomiak, to be tried and eventually hanged for four murders, claims her attention: "The lad looks about sixteen but they say he is nineteen. He says that he did not mean to kill Doak but just shot to wound him and force retaliation." On the return journey south on the Mackenzie, an Inuit woman, Laura, who was being forced to Edmonton to appear before Justice Murphy and possibly confined as insane for having beaten her husband, gains MGE's sympathy. "I suggested that perhaps the husband needed beating up," she observes. Tints of admiration colour her portrait of Laura:

Top: Alex Stefansson and two of his pals, Aklavik [magic lantern slide] 96-91 MGE S1

Bottom: Alex Stefansson, Aklavik [magic lantern slide] 96-91 MGE S1

First Inuit Condemned and Executed

Inuit hunters **Alikomiak and Tàtimagana were arrested for the murder of four Inuit at Coronation Gulf in 1921. While in custody at Tree River, Alikomiak shot and killed RCMP officer W.A. Doak and Hudson's Bay Company employee Otto Binder. Both were sentenced to death; despite pleas for leniency, they were hanged in an abandoned whaling shed on Herschel Island (1 February 1924).**

> All day she sits or stands out on the side deck, rolling cigarettes and smoking. When she gets tired standing, she sits flat down on the floor with her legs straight out in front like a baby. That would be a new one to add to the 'daily dozen' and warranted to strengthen the back.

Left: Alikomiak at Fort McPherson [magic lantern slide] 96-91 MGE S1

Ellis is happy to report parenthetically that Laura was "found mentally all right and sent back, her worst fault seeming to be that she was an inveterate smoker and also drank when the opportunity offered." She encounters and relates tales of survival, like the Pittsburgh native who suffered gangrene, eventually amputated his own toes with a jackknife, and survived alone for over four months with only twenty-five pounds of flour, which he mixed with snow, and who now does not want to leave the North.

Thanks to Ellis's keen eye, "Down North" is equally adept at documenting topographical conditions. Her text has prescient observations on the oil sands, "regular mountains of asphalt," used at the time for superior road surfaces, as one day "going to mean millions of dollars to

Left: "Laura" [magic lantern slide] 96-91 MGE S1

Right: "McCleary, Fort Norman, the man who was so badly frozen" [magic lantern slide] 96-91 MGE S1

General features

REPRINTED FROM THE FAMILY HERALD AND WEEKLY STAR
MONTREAL, CANADA, APRIL 13, 1932

ASPHALT FROM NORTH FOR ROAD PAVING

Pure salt evaporated from the briny water near Fort Smith

Cassette Rapids near Fort Smith make necessary a portage of eighteen miles

By MIRIAM GREEN ELLIS

WESTERN CANADA was first known to the world for its fur; then the ranchers came in and pastured their cattle and horses and sheep on large indefinite areas in the Southern parts; the next step was the growing of wheat on very definite areas across the centre and south, and Western Canada wheat still holds its own in world markets as does the Northern fur. But the fur country is coming to the front again in quite another manner. Under the soil are magnificent resources of which little was known until recent years when the extent of the pitchblende deposits from which comes the super valuable radium, has made front page news for the North Country. Its silver, copper, iron, lead, zinc and gold deposits are found to be very valuable; there is enough asphalt to pave all the roads that Canada will ever have and still have some to spare; there are great quantities of pulp and salt not to mention fish which are being shipped out by train load to Chicago and other big centres.

It is prophesied that in a few years the banks of the Athabaska river will be lined with smoke stacks. There are three main industries which may be developed in this area, one piled on top of the other—first, the pulpwood; roll that away and there are the oily masses of the asphalt sands, underneath which is limestone and salt. There is probably no better site in America for a large paper industry, considering the cheap water power, the immense pulp supply, salt for making soda ash which is largely used in paper making and limestone for making sulphite paper. Also there is asphalt to be extracted from these bituminous sands for making building paper; shingles may be added to complete the industry.

The asphalt sands rest on Devonian limestone, one of the finest specimens of building stone in the country. It is beautifully mottled with brown fossils and below this is a 200 foot strata of one of the purest salt deposits to be found in America.

As a paving material the "Alberta Tar Sands" have a high standing, and long before anyone thought of roads in Canada, the Indians were using this sticky material that oozed out of the river bank on a hot day, for caulking their canoes.

They are mis-named "Tar Sands," since this is an asphaltic material, not tar which is a product of coal. The area is about 300 miles north and east of Edmonton over the Watershed.

From the foothills of the Rockies come the

freight on the bulk is saved and accurate mixtures are assured.

Thomas Draper, manager of the McMurray Asphalt and Oil Company, who has been working on this material for a great many years believes that the material as it is mined with every grain of sand thoroughly coated with the oils is a better base on which to work. So in his paving he mixes the "Tar Sands" with an equal amount of sand or gravel. As stated before the content of the sands varies very greatly, so before leaving the plant at McMurray, he brings the composition to the point where it needs just equal measure for measure with sand and gravel. The whole amount is then heated to 300 degrees to allow all the added aggregate to be thoroughly coated with the surplus asphalt.

The Mines Branch, Ottawa, has made topographical surveys of the extensive areas, has examined and sampled the principal outcrops and also mined trial shipments and made demonstration pavements as well as studying methods of recovering the bitumen from the crude sands. Sidney C. Ellis, of the Mines Branch, is one of those who believe the bitumen should be extracted before shipment. The Geological department of the University of Alberta has also done considerable investigation in this work, also the Research Council of Canada.

There is no doubt in the minds of any of these investigators that in the "Alberta Tar Sands" Canada has a wonderful natural resource. Its immensity is rather staggering. Mr. Ellis has found outcrops of the bituminous sands along the Athabaska river and its principal tributaries for a total distance of more than 220 miles. The area which it covers is approximately 115 miles north and south and 45 miles east and west.

The cliffs where the Draper Company is

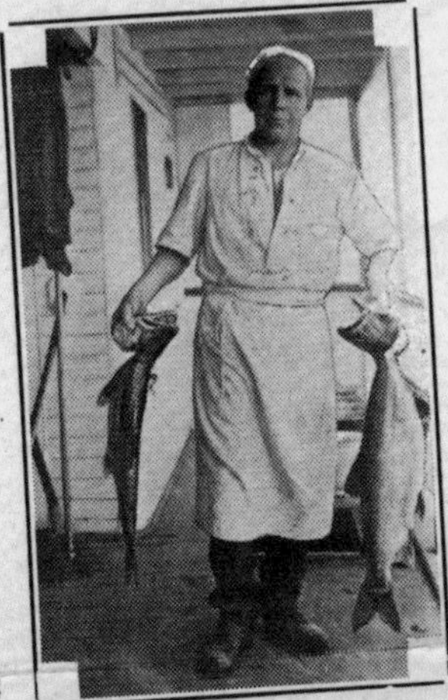

Among the natural resources of the North are the trout and other fish of Great Slave Lake

ing from frost and impervious to rain so that the base is thoroughly protected.

One of the strong claims for the asphalt sands is that it does protect the base and thus saves at least 50 per cent of the cost of a new road. As good gravel for roads becomes more and more scarce, the importance of salvaging it on the roads is more important. On the ordinary much travelled gravel highway an inch or so of gravel is ground up and blown away every year or so. Surfacing with the asphalt conserves the gravel indefinitely.

The use of small simple machines makes

Tar sands lowered from top of cliff by inclined road

Ponoka and other towns and villages in Alberta.

Back in 1914 the Dominion Government laid down a stretch of this asphalt on the Fort Road in Edmonton. It has preserved splendidly. In the spring thaws, it may heave, but it stretches like elastic and does not break.

Reductions in freight tariffs have been secured and the asphalt has been shipped as far

Left:
"Asphalt from North for Road Paving"
FHWS 12 April 1932
96-91 MGE 11.I

Right:
Woman with child [magic lantern slide]
96-91 MGE S1

the country"; despite the opinion of the "cracker-box orators" on board, "squelching one's enthusiasms" that "it was 'just some fool scratching round in the dirt,'" Ellis maintains her "visions of another Klondyke." She documents Native women's importance in preparing hides, befriends Native families, notes features of dress, childcare, and diet, and records Native delight in taking pictures of the White

She documents Native women's importance in
preparing hides, befriends Native families,
notes features of dress, childcare, and
diet, and records Native delight in taking
pictures of the White visitors.

This page: various images of women and families [magic lantern slides] 96-91 MGE S1

Facing page: Loucheux at Fort McPherson [magic lantern slide] 96-91 MGE S1

Access to Family Life

Language barriers did not prevent MGE from establishing communication with First Nations women. The interior scene of a two-day-old baby in a hammock at Fort Norman conveys a remarkable ease and closeness. At Fort McPherson, scraping caribou hides is the woman's livelihood. Although the children in the Aklavik photo are shy, their mothers are more intrigued.

Above: Fort Simpson operating room [photo album]
96-91 MGE 1.III

Circle: Suffering from blistered feet at Salt Springs [photo album]
96-91 MGE 1.II

visitors. As well as entering mission schools and churches and investigating operating-room procedures, such as the one at Fort Simpson, she relays endearing exuberance and vulnerability, piloting the boat for thirty miles beyond Fort Chipewyan and taking a daily swim in the Mackenzie, admitting to anxiety about mounting her first horse—"I cannot understand why they put the stirrups up so high"—and, at Salt Springs, a thirty-seven–mile journey inland, revealing the perils of a tenderfoot who suffers blisters.

A strong-willed personality suffuses every page of "Down North." From the outset Ellis chafes at her editor's apparent lack of interest in her proposed trip to the North Pole, as the opening episode in early spring illustrates.

> One day I sat in the Premier's office trying to get a 'scoop' on the government policy in connection with the administration of the liquor laws, when I noticed on his

desk a pamphlet from a transportation company, on which were the words "To the land of the midnight sun." From where I sat in that big blue room, I could see the North Saskatchewan River, just then throwing off its winter bondage and shoving the great cakes of ice ignominiously on the shore to rot. The trees were showing life and the grass along the banks was getting green. It was the time the woods sent out their loudest call, and I lost all interest in the burning question of liquor laws.

Centre: "Swimming The Great Mackenzie River, Arctic Circle" [photo album] MGE 96-91 1.III

Above left: Salt Springs [magic lantern slide] 96-91 MGE S1

Above right: Horse patrol at Salt Springs [photo album] 96-91 MGE 1.III

She also strikes a blow for women in breeches, but not without a shamefaced admission. Having "put on [her] knickers and big boots ... with a defiant air," Ellis is "anxious to see what was behind that screen of trees, ... to penetrate the leafy foliage." For one time only does she accede to the captain's directive "that he could not think of allowing me to leave the boat," but quickly vows "that it won't happen again." Her oath, along with the polemical comment that such a concession indicates "why women do not deserve equal rights," packs conviction: "That man is about half as big as I am and I should just have taken him by the collar and thrown him overboard."

Right: Sunset [magic lantern slide] 96-91 MGE S1

Bottom: "Orchids found on island in Great Slave Lake" 96-91 MGE 3.IV

Her trips ashore have a less pugnacious tone, showing an observant naturalist at work. The discovery of wild orchids, "the most exquisite things I ever saw," reminds her of "fairies' graves." Blue-eyed grass, lupines, tea berries, wild strawberries, and the omnipresent pink, rose, and purple drooping blossoms of the *Heydesarum mackenzii* merit detailed description. So do the "never-ending" sunsets, "liquid light lying on the water," "a bright rich amber, shading to yellow gold." The prospect of a return journey along narrower and shallower rivers, unlike the majesty of the Mackenzie, occasions sadness: "it was like the slow unfurling of a great banner, and now we are rolling it up again till it will be just an uninteresting stick."

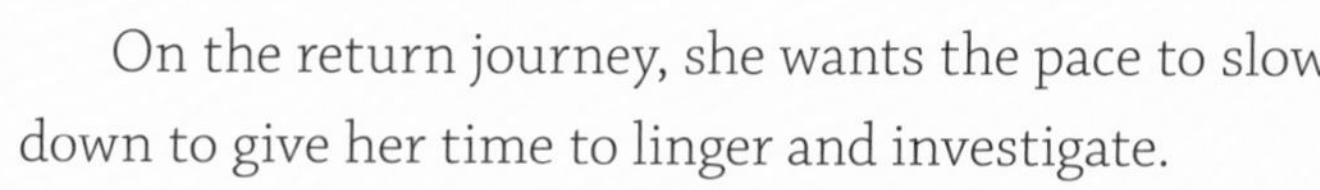

On the return journey, she wants the pace to slow down to give her time to linger and investigate.

> July 15—We are racing to get to Fort Smith before the boat leaves the other end of the portage for Waterways. Personally I am hoping we miss it, for I want a few days to wander around Smith and I am sick of being rushed. However I don't dare mention this as everyone else is fairly tense with the fear that we shall not make connections.
>
> July 17—Thank heaven we missed that boat and now I will have three days.
>
> July 18—Again thank heaven we missed the boat for when I thought everything was past, the 'big adventure' still awaits me. All down these thousands of miles of river banks, I have wanted to get in behind the curtain of trees that formed such an effective screen along the edge, and see the life, birds, beast, flower, or human, whatever it were.

"Down North, 1922," likely composed in the fall of that year and mined successively thereafter for newspaper articles and magic lantern lectures, is a significant and singular contribution to women's travel accounts dealing

Main street at Waterways
[photo album] 96-91 MGE 1.III

with Western Canada and the Arctic. Its distinctive immediacy emerging from Ellis's journalism experience, "Down North" also stands apart from the published records of earlier and contemporary women recreational adventurers or professional travel writers, who were supported by family wealth, industrial sponsors, or employed, attending husbands. The personal voice, the occasional humiliation, and the encounter with a wide social spectrum separate Ellis's work from the amateur Victorian travelogues of the wives of serving or future Canadian governors general detailing their cross-country visits with the elite of the Dominion: the Marchioness

Loucheux couple, Fort McPherson
[magic lantern slide] 96-91 MGE S1

of Dufferin and Ava's *My Canadian Journal, 1872–78, Extracts from My Letters Home* (1891) and the Marchioness of Aberdeen's *Through Canada with a Kodak* (1893). Though incomplete (or at least unconcluded), Ellis's account is fuller than the report of the American Elizabeth Taylor, a self-taught botanist and collector for museums, who travelled down the Mackenzie in 1892 with the permission of the Governor of the Hudson's Bay Company, publishing brief essays two and five years later in *Outing* and *Travel*. Later records of travel show considerably less travail than Ellis's account. Jean Walker Godsell's description of her 1920 honeymoon trip north as a Hudson's Bay Company factor's wife, in *I Was No Lady* (1959), sketches "God's Wide Open Spaces where men were men and where white women were placed on pedestals since they were few in number and far between" (Godsell 2). Clara (Roger) Vyvyan's 1926 journey by steamer, motor boat, and canoe to Alaska published thirty-five years later as *Arctic Adventure* (1961), a carefully planned and guided trip, reflects the aspirations of a well-to-do, middle-aged Englishwoman and her female artist-companion, who read Shakespeare to one another en route.

Dedicated Observers

At Fort McPherson **MGE was clearly struck by this Loucheux man and wife. She annotated this beautifully composed photo with the information she had gleaned about its subjects: "He is blind but watches the boat just the same."**

Beyond the Beckoning Border

WITH

AGNES DEANS CAMERON

FIVE TRAVEL-TALKS ON WESTERN AND NORTHERN CANADA BY THE VICE-PRESIDENT OF THE CANADIAN WOMEN'S PRESS CLUB

EACH TALK IS ILLUSTRATED BY ONE HUNDRED DISTINCT STEREOPTICON VIEWS FROM THE TRAVELLER'S OWN CAMERA

1—**BETWEEN THE GATES OF CANADA.** A trip by rail from Atlantic to Pacific across the trans-continental spine of Canada, with steppings-aside along the short ribs and long ribs.

2—**WHEAT, THE WIZARD OF THE NORTH.** The Story of Canada's Wheat Belt, a bread-yielding plain as large as Europe. Here new cities rise in the night, and surging into the fat mesas come people from the world's four corners. It is the Melting-Pot of the Nations.

3—**FROM WHEAT TO WHALES.** The Story of Agnes Deans Cameron's Ten Thousand-Mile Journey from Chicago to the Arctic by way of the Athabasca, Great Slave Lake and Mighty Mackenzie, with word-pictures of Crees, Chipewyans, Dog-Ribs, Yellow-Knives, Mounted Police, Fur-Traders, Cloistered Nuns and fur-clad Eskimo.

4—**THE WITCHERY OF THE PEACE.** Miss Cameron's Journey from the Eskimo in the Arctic, homeward by way of the Peace River and the Lesser Slave, with stories of the Chutes of the Peace, Moose-Hunting, the Golden Grain-Fields of Vermilion, America's most northerly Flour-Mill, Alexander Mackenzie's Last Camp, and Cannibal Louise the Wentigo.

5—**VANCOUVER'S ISLE O' DREAMS.** The most cosmopolitan island in the world, half the size of troubled Ireland, with her Sealing-Fleets, Whale-Fisheries, Salmon Weirs, 300-foot Pines, Wonder-Mines, Apple Orchards, Christmas Roses, and cultured people.

The journey most comparable to Ellis's is Agnes Deans Cameron's arrival at Fort Rae in 1908, recounted in *The New North* (1909), a text that Ellis's informal history of the CWPC reveals she knew. "That book came back at me like a boomerang," Ellis revealed to her Edmonton audience.

> When I went down the Mackenzie in 1922, the natives clammed up on me when I said I wanted to write about them. Seems Cameron had borrowed precious photographs and failed to return them, as promised. ("Pathfinders" 8)

Ellis was clearly familiar with the earlier account while she was travelling. Fourteen years after Cameron, she visits one of the residents of Fort McMurray mentioned extensively in *The New North*, Christina Gordon. On July 25 Miriam's diary relates a meeting with this Scottish free trader who gives her visitor "lettuce out of a splendid

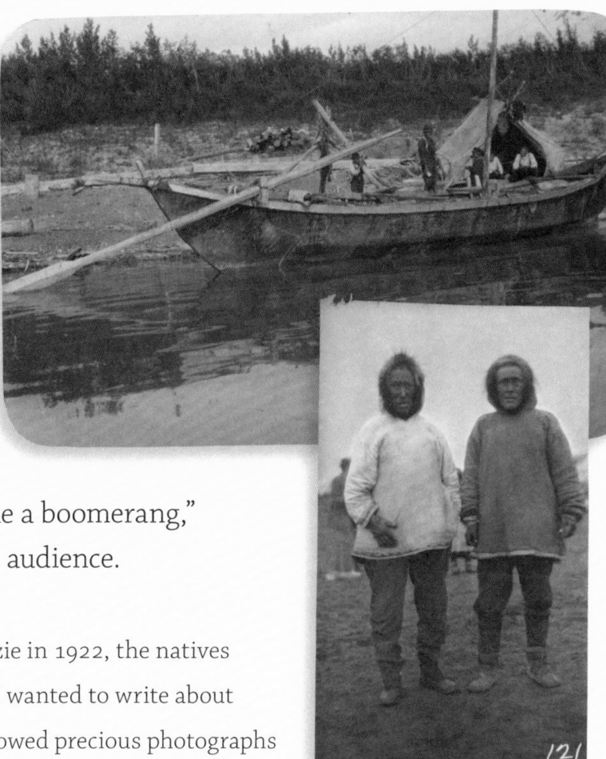

Left: Promotional material for lectures by Agnes Deans Cameron (Courtesy Provincial Archives of Alberta PA1974 0056/5)

Above left: Skin boat, Fort Norman [magic lantern slide] 96-91 MGE S1

Above right: "Eskimos in their snow shirts" [magic lantern slide] 96-91 MGE S1

Christina Gordon in garden at Fort McMurray [photo album] 96-91 MGE 1.III

> She is sort of washed out but was very interested in the fact that Miss Cameron had put her in her book and had lectured about her in London. She had been sent many books from the publishers and when she had the post office had given these to the bachelors who had come for mail and were going away disappointed because none had come. (Diary, July 25, 169)

garden" (169). Changes in situation and attitude separate the two accounts. In 1908 Cameron was proud to introduce the fur trader as "operating in opposition to the great and only Hudson's Bay Company" (Cameron 84), while by the time of her visit Ellis notes that "the H. B. store has taken over" Gordon's role as postmistress. Admiring Gordon's concern for local bachelors pining for mail, Ellis relates matter-of-factly the practical use to which this sensible and now-aging Scot puts the complimentary copies of *The New North*:

With each of its twenty-four chapters headed by a literary or biblical epigraph, *The New North* is a precisely worded, photo-illustrated narrative of close to four hundred pages, tessellated with passages of strenuous didacticism, recounting the journey of Cameron and her niece, an accommodating typist, from Chicago to the North, via stagecoach, scow, steamer, and paddle-wheeler, with a return terminus in Winnipeg. Although she served as vice-president of the CWPC, Cameron (1863–1912) was not officially a press woman; rather, as a teacher for twenty-five years and the first woman high-school principal in Victoria, she had run afoul of the school board trustees and been dismissed. Journalism in Chicago and the trip north, along with its resultant lectures in Canada and the United States, and talks in Britain promoting immigration, provided her livelihood before her untimely death. In the opinion of Anglican missionary Archdeacon Charles Whittaker, *The New North* was "an intricate compound of fact and fiction" (MacLaren and LaFramboise xxix).

While differences in length and aim between a published volume and a typescript are evident contrasts, so too are the personalities conveyed in the writing. Accustomed to lecturing in a classroom and acutely conscious of her role as instructive authority rather than curious observer, Cameron is quick to impart anthropological lessons. Ellis seems more eager to talk to people and hear their stories. After the forty-five–mile width of the Mackenzie River, passage through the spectacular banks of limestone cliffs at the Ramparts, where the width narrows to less than a half mile at the entrance to Fort Good Hope, provokes a lengthy Romantic description from Cameron. Though enjoying

Above: R.C. Mission church at Fort Good Hope decorated by Émile Petitot, OMI [magic lantern slide]
96-91 MGE S1

Left: Ramparts on the Mackenzie River at the entrance to Fort Good Hope [magic lantern slide]
96-91 MGE S1

Packing Cases for "Land of the Midnight Sun" lectures
96-91 MGE 4 & 5

This page and facing page:
Assorted magic lantern slides 96-91 MGE S1; assorted negatives 96-91 MGE 6

the rarity of typing without light well past midnight, Ellis finds herself, by contrast, silenced and awed in face of the beauty around her.

The kinds of promotional tours resulting from both trips also underscore the contrasts. For paying audiences in the thousands across Canada and in Illinois and Minnesota, Cameron organized five detailed lectures with snappy titles, under the general banner "Beyond the Beckoning Border," all extracted from her recently released book. Less lavish, Ellis's lecture, entitled "The Land of the Midnight Sun," was "a magic journey"; as the *Toronto Telegram* reported, "she used her eyes well, and her delicious sense of humour and keen love of real human beings made her lecture a joy" ("Cornelia").

Above: Loucheux women at Fort McPherson [magic lantern slide] 96-91 MGE S1

Facing page: "Finnigan Jr. and The Toad" [photo album] 96-91 MGE 1.II

Focus on Women

THE AKLAVIK TRIP established MGE's career on a strong upward trajectory. Magic lantern lectures, placement of the NWT journey stories in a variety of venues, and landing the plum position of Western Editor for the *Family Herald and Weekly Star* all followed. One feature connecting her work throughout early, secure, and post-retirement phases is her unwavering commitment to telling women's stories.

While MGE's sympathetic support of farm wives organizing for suffrage, for local nurses, and for well-run rural schools was immediate and long-lasting, she was also adept at confessing aspects of her own struggles with machinery, train schedules, and the dictates of feminine fashion. She made the account of learning to drive in 1915 into an entertaining article, "My Car 'Finnigan' and I," for the *Grain Growers' Guide* (7 April 1920). "'You can try your driving'" appear to be the last words MGE heard from her husband, as he left her in their car at the barracks in Prince Albert. The emphasis in the article is not on the abruptness of the farewell—and it does sound curt—but rather on the consequences for a woman alone behind the wheel of a second-hand motor car. With the help of a gallant "young captain," she manages to get the car started and admits, "I got away then, and I never stopped that whole morning, partly from fear I would not get started again, and partly because I was determined to overcome my fear about driving that car before I let it out of my hands." The finicky, temperamental auto, nicknamed "Finnigan" in honour of American humorist Strickland W. Gillilan's verse about an Irish railwayman who reports derailments as "off agin, on agin, gone agin—Finnigin," lives up to its unpredictable namesake. MGE's account of changing tires in the rain underlines the requirement of a well-developed "auxiliary vocabulary."

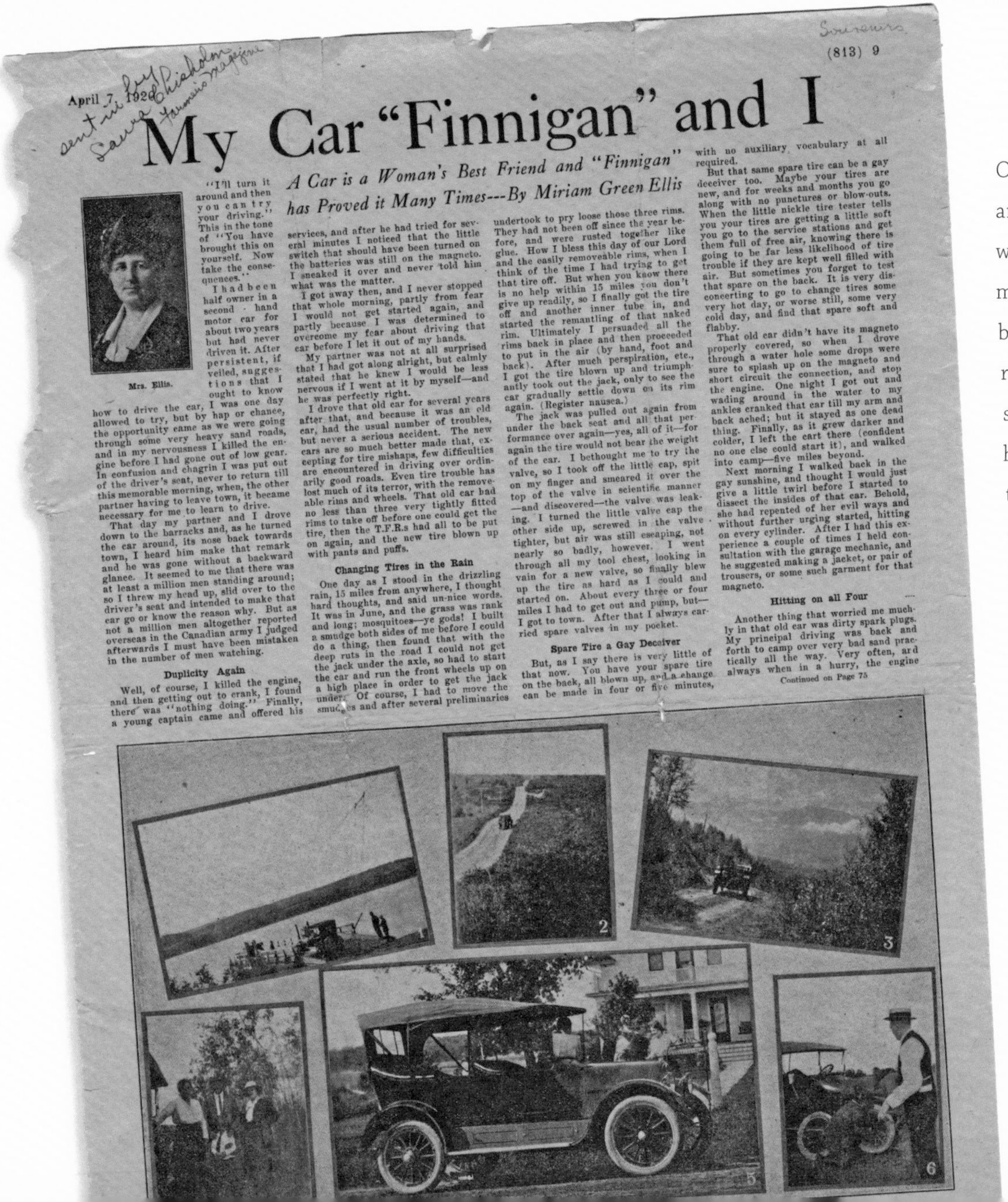

April 7, 1920 (813) 9

My Car "Finnigan" and I

A Car is a Woman's Best Friend and "Finnigan" has Proved it Many Times---By Miriam Green Ellis

Mrs. Ellis.

"I'll turn it around and then you can try your driving." This in the tone of "You have brought this on yourself. Now take the consequences."

I had been half owner in a second-hand motor car for about two years but had never driven it. After persistent, if veiled, suggestions that I ought to know how to drive the car, I was one day allowed to try, but by hap or chance, the opportunity came as we were going through some very heavy sand roads, and in my nervousness I killed the engine before I had gone out of low gear. In confusion and chagrin I was put out of the driver's seat, never to return till this memorable morning, when, the other partner having to leave town, it became necessary for me to learn to drive.

That day my partner and I drove down to the barracks and, as he turned the car around, its nose back towards town, I heard him make that remark and he was gone without a backward glance. It seemed to me that there was at least a million men standing around; so I threw my head up, slid over to the driver's seat and intended to make that car go or know the reason why. But as not a million men altogether reported overseas in the Canadian army I judged afterwards I must have been mistaken in the number of men watching.

Duplicity Again

Well, of course, I killed the engine, and then getting out to crank, I found there was "nothing doing." Finally, a young captain came and offered his services, and after he had tried for several minutes I noticed that the little switch that should have been turned on the batteries was still on the magneto. I sneaked it over and never told him what was the matter.

I got away then, and I never stopped that whole morning, partly from fear I would not get started again, and partly because I was determined to overcome my fear about driving that car before I let it out of my hands.

My partner was not at all surprised that I had got along alright, but calmly stated that he knew I would be less nervous if I went at it by myself—and he was perfectly right.

I drove that old car for several years after that, and because it was an old car, had the usual number of troubles, but never a serious accident. The new cars are so much better made that, excepting for tire mishaps, few difficulties are encountered in driving over ordinarily good roads. Even tire trouble has lost much of its terror, with the removeable rims and wheels. That old car had no less than three very tightly fitted rims to take off before one could get the tire, then the T.F.R.s had all to be put on again, and the new tire blown up with pants and puffs.

Changing Tires in the Rain

One day as I stood in the drizzling rain, 15 miles from anywhere, I thought hard thoughts, and said un-nice words. It was in June, and the grass was rank and long; mosquitoes—ye gods! I built a smudge both sides of me before I could do a thing, then found that with the deep ruts in the road I could not get the jack under the axle, so had to start the car and run the front wheels up on a high place in order to get the jack under. Of course, I had to move the smudges and after several preliminaries undertook to pry loose those three rims. They had not been off since the year before, and were rusted together like glue. How I bless this day of our Lord and the easily removeable rims, when I think of the time I had trying to get that tire off. But when you know there is no help within 15 miles you don't give up readily, so I finally got the tire off and another inner tube in, and started the remantling of that naked rim. Ultimately I persuaded all the rims back in place and then proceeded to put in the air (by hand, foot and back). After much perspiration, etc., I got the tire blown up and triumphantly took out the jack, only to see the car gradually settle down on its rim again. (Register nausea.)

The jack was pulled out again from under the back seat and all that performance over again—yes, all of it—for again the tire would not bear the weight of the car. I bethought me to try the valve, so I took off the little cap, spit on my finger and smeared it over the top of the valve in scientific manner—and discovered—the valve was leaking. I turned the little valve cap the other side up, screwed in the valve tighter, but air was still escaping, not nearly so badly, however. I went through all my tool chest, looking in vain for a new valve, so finally blew up the tire as hard as I could and started on. About every three or four miles I had to get out and pump, but—I got to town. After that I always carried spare valves in my pocket.

Spare Tire a Gay Deceiver

But, as I say there is very little of that now. You have your spare tire on the back, all blown up, and a change can be made in four or five minutes, with no auxiliary vocabulary at all required.

But that same spare tire can be a gay deceiver too. Maybe your tires are new, and for weeks and months you go along with no punctures or blow-outs. When the little nickle tire tester tells you your tires are getting a little soft you go to the service stations and get them full of free air, knowing there is going to be far less likelihood of tire trouble if they are kept well filled with air. But sometimes you forget to test that spare on the back. It is very disconcerting to go to change tires some very hot day, or worse still, some very cold day, and find that spare soft and flabby.

That old car didn't have its magneto properly covered, so when I drove through a water hole some drops were sure to splash up on the magneto and short circuit the connection, and stop the engine. One night I got out and wading around in the water to my ankles cranked that car till my arm and back ached; but it stayed as one dead thing. Finally, as it grew darker and colder, I left the cart there (confident no one else could start it), and walked into camp—five miles beyond.

Next morning I walked back in the gay sunshine, and thought I would just give a little twirl before I started to dissect the insides of that car. Behold, she had repented of her evil ways and without further urging started, hitting on every cylinder. After I had this experience a couple of times I held consultation with the garage mechanic, and he suggested making a jacket, or pair of trousers, or some such garment for that magneto.

Hitting on all Four

Another thing that worried me muchly in that old car was dirty spark plugs. My principal driving was back and forth to camp over very bad sand practically all the way. Very often, and always when in a hurry, the engine

Continued on Page 75

One day as I stood in the drizzling rain, 15 miles from anywhere, I thought hard thoughts and said un-nice words. It was in June, and the grass was rank and long; mosquitoes—ye gods! I built a smudge both sides of me before I could do a thing, then found that with the deep ruts in the road I could not get the jack under the axle, so had to start the car and run the front wheels up on a high place in order to get the jack under. Of course I had to move the smudges and after several preliminaries undertook to pry loose those three rims. They had not been off since the year before, and were rusted together like glue. How I bless this day of our Lord and the easily removeable rims, when I think of the time I had trying to get that tire off. But when you know there is no help within 15 miles you don't give up readily, so I finally got the tire off and another inner tube in, and started the remantling of that naked rim. Ultimately I persuaded all the rims back in place and then proceeded to put in the air (by hand, foot, and back). After much perspiration, etc., I got the tire blown up and triumphantly took out the jack, only to see the car gradually settle down on its rim again. (Register nausea.)

Left: "My Car 'Finnigan' and I" *Grain Grower's Guide* 7 April 1920 96-91 MGE 2.1

The jack was pulled out again from under the back seat and all that performance over again—yes, all of it—for again the tire would not bear the weight of the car. I bethought me to try the valve, so I took off the little cap, spit on my finger and smeared it over the top of the valve in scientific manner—and discovered—the valve was leaking. I turned the little valve cap the other side up, screwed in the valve tighter, but air was still escaping, not nearly so badly, however. I went through all my tool-chest, looking in vain for a new valve, so finally blew up the tire as hard as I could and started on. About every three or four miles I had to get out and pump, but—I got to town. After that I always carried spare valves in my pocket.

To the University Women's Club in Saskatoon MGE revealed another challenging moment, after having covered a story in south-central Alberta.

Late in the evening I got to Olds, got a room at the hotel, and left a call for 3 a.m. I hesitated whether I would undress or just lie down on the bed, but decided on the undressing. When I got up at 3 a.m., I hated to think of the effort of dressing and walking across the street to the station, getting in a train, and undressing again for another two hours sleep. So finally decided, since there would be no one on the street at that hour anyway, that I would just put my slicker over my pajamas and carry my clothes. I

A Welcomed Visitor

Miriam had a truly engaging and ecumenical curiosity. **She visited Anglican and Catholic churches and missions. At Fort Resolution, although the founding superior, Soeur Alice McQuillan, SGM, was on holiday in New Brunswick, Miriam was greeted by Sister St. Rose, and there was an evident fondness between the two women. In her diary entry for June 29, Miriam records: "Sister St. Rose gave me some cakes and cookies with red sugar for my birthday." Miriam also notes that she spent the night reading *The Grey Nuns of the Far North*, a monograph by Pierre Duchassois, OMI, published in 1919.**

Sister St. Rose, Fort Resolution
[magic lantern slide] 96-91 MGE S1

Left: MGE at Leduc [magic lantern slide] 96-91 MGE S1

Right: Emily Murphy photo from *Should Auld Acquaintance Be Forgot* 96-91 MGE 1.V

> tried to stuff my pajama legs into my stockings, but they were those large sailor-type and would not go. By this time I could hear the train whistle, so I grabbed up my clothes and sailed across the street to the station with mustard-coloured pajamas flying in the wind.

A biplane trip to Lac La Ronge, north of Prince Albert, brings up the embarrassing "skirt business" and the difficulties of maintaining "modest pride ... as you sort of straddled up from one side to the other on these two rods" of the Model T plane, a difficulty she overcomes by wearing slacks on the return.

MGE reserved non-ironic praise for farm women, whom she described to the Rotary Ladies of Yorkton as "the shock troops." Her writing is tessellated with commendations of their courage and determination, in keeping with the views of her staunch Edmonton friends Emily Murphy and Nellie McClung. In *Janey Canuck in the West* (1910) Emily [Ferguson] Murphy summed up the demands on the Western farm woman nicely as being "a combination of Mary, Martha, Magdalen, Bridget, and the Queen of Sheba" (Ferguson 74). Women's lot was severe, Nellie McClung recalled in the second volume of her autobiography, *The Stream Runs Fast* (1945). As well as "all their hard work and

their strivings to keep clean and make a decent living for themselves and their families," she noted, the women have still "the additional burden of child-bearing"; the situations she saw were not glamorous:

> These little houses are places where people have the minimum of comfort. They go in and out, eat and sleep, but everything's done the hard way. The women are tired and overworked and sometimes very cross. They battle against hard water and chapped hands, and chapped hands would lower the morale of an arch-angel. The houses are cold, the floors full of splinters. (McClung 210)

Yet in the midst of these challenges—and, arguably, because of them—a remarkable solidarity among prairie rural women moved them "to sign temperance petitions, to contribute their mite to women's missionary societies, to agitate for the vote, and to demand recognition of women's right to employment and the value of their domestic labour" (Strong-Boag 403).

When she covered the second annual meeting of the Women Grain Growers of Saskatchewan for *Woman's Century* in 1915, MGE lauded their aims of "social betterment, educational uplift, a broader business basis for their work, more aesthetic surroundings, and for rights and privileges as women and human beings." Practical actions were key:

> They are keenly interested in the education of their children under proper conditions and with proper surroundings. They are trying to make arrangements for providing nurses in the country districts where women could not afford properly qualified nurses from the cities. They are also making arrangements for travelling libraries.

The Women Grain Growers' engagement "in all matters that interest women" impressed MGE as the hallmark of their forward-looking enterprise.

> They thoroughly appreciated Miss Cora Hind's address on 'Made-in-Canada,' and it would be hard for anyone not to enjoy such a practical, concise presentation of this business woman's views.

Miriam Green Ellis

Photo from *Should Auld Acquaintance Be Forgot*. "A Recipe for Remembrance" to Jane Stewart from the Edmonton Women's Press Club. 10 June 1922 96-91 MGE 1.V

E. Cora Hind [photo album] 96-91 MGE 1.II

> The Women Grain Growers were especially keen on the addresses about Equal Franchise, Women's Rights, etc. In fact, it was at the insistent demands of these women's locals that their Provincial Executive took up the matter of presenting a suffrage petition to Parliament. ... Their interests are as wide as they are varied, and only good can come of their splendid organization, which stands above all for co-operation.

In calling women "shock troops," MGE noted their ability "to get the children soothed down before father gets home, ... adjust the household to meet an onslaught of in-laws, [and] out in the country [to] milk the cows and feed the calves, while father goes to a convention." The context for this 1939 talk to the Rotary Ladies of Yorkton is conventionally domestic and patriarchal. She stressed woman's adaptability as well: "When funds get low she makes over her wedding dress so her daughter can go to a party. If worse comes to worse, she makes flour sacks into under clothing, taking care to put on a little pretty embroidery." But for these same listeners, MGE, who never had to soothe children, redesign a wedding dress, or concoct lingerie from flour sacks, could enact roles of praise and critique. Capable managers and domestic mainstays, women incarnate "a tremendous wealth of stability, initiative and energy"; yet she interrupted her plaudits with the qualifier that this wealth "isn't working to capacity." "Women fought hard to get the vote," she noted, "but having it they lay back on their laurels."

Left: Mrs. Conibear at Fort Smith [magic lantern slide] 96-91 MGE S1

Whether the women she wrote about were striving entrepreneurs like Mrs. Conibear, with her well-stocked and expanding trading post at Fort Smith, or the unnamed farm wife who accommodated MGE overnight in a one-room shack, Ellis is impressed by their tenacious determination—adding to commercial success or facing unutterable loss. The account of the overnight stay MGE glanced at in her 1939 talk at Yorkton emerges as a full article almost two decades later, in a post-retirement piece for the *Western Producer*. In "Memorable Stopping Place" (19 June 1958), she supplies more recollected detail of the time when "there were few hotels in the country":

> One afternoon, in a new settlement northwest of Edmonton which was then being reclaimed from the bush, but which is now probably covered with oil derricks, I asked for supper and bed at a small log shack. I had heard of this place with the recommendation that it was clean (meaning no bed bugs) and that the teacher lived there. They hesitated, explaining it was merely a one-room place with a tiny lean-to for a summer kitchen; one corner was curtained off with a sheet for the teacher. They did not have much food, she said.

As night was coming on I put on a little pressure; in those pioneering days, people knew what it meant to need a place to spend the night. Having taken me in, the man and his wife moved out to a bit of barn where the cow lived in the winter and their small pale son slept on a couple of chairs close to my bed.

As the woman churns butter and makes baking powder biscuits, Miriam learns her story.

As she paced back and forth churning her cream, I found that they had come from the Western States after having gone broke entirely at the past place. When they arrived in Alberta, they did not even have a team of horses left, nothing but their trunk, enough money to put down on a homestead and buy an axe and one or two tools and some flour. They built the shack and went into town to work for the winter to buy a grubstake. This had gone on for several winters, the summers being spent on the homestead 'proving up.' They were required by law to spend six months of the year on the land and making certain improvements.

Washing dishes together after "extraordinarily good eating" leads to more revelations about their sad struggles.

Several winters they spent in town waiting on tables or shovelling snow or whatever was to be done to earn cash. Then the babies started to come and she had to stay home while the husband still went to town for they needed money more than ever. All the time they were holding tenaciously to the homestead and 'a home of their own.'

Then one winter as she stayed home alone with the children, diphtheria struck. She never knew where the bug came from, but one after another, the children sickened and died. The ground was frozen solid, she could not dig graves for her babies so she just laid them out in the lean-to shed where the little bodies were frozen solid in a few minutes. There they were till her husband came home in the spring.

Pregnant again and "utterly refusing to take money for the service she had rendered," this woman causes Miriam to sleep fitfully.

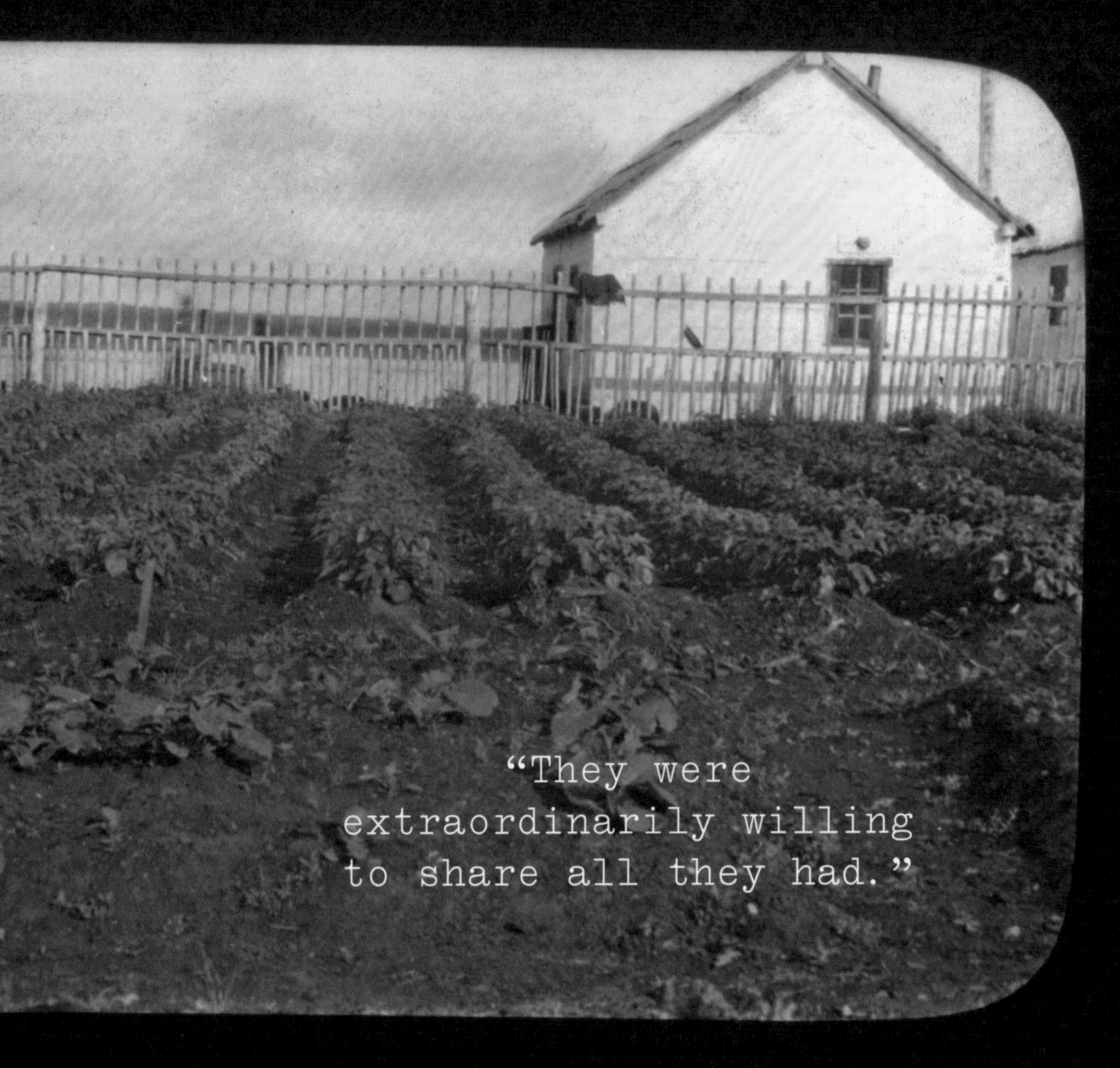
"They were extraordinarily willing to share all they had."

> That night as I laid on their home-made bed, with its straw tick scratching me as I moved, I thought a lot of this little family; the father and mother lying out in the dug-out to give me their bed; the anemic little boy, and I hated myself for eating that butter which he needed so much more than I did.

As the woman, grateful for "having someone to talk to" and for "the papers and magazines," bids her farewell, Miriam remarks on this humbling generosity: "They were extraordinarily willing to share all they had and were in no way repaid by the bill I managed to slip into the lad's collar, as I drove away quickly before they saw it."

"Potatoes at Fort Good Hope"
[magic lantern slide] 96-91 MGE S1

Covering a Changing West

ALERT TO SHIFTS AND MOMENTOUS EVENTS on the land and keen to offer informed forecasts of developments in the offing, MGE always concentrated on a human, individual perspective. The reporter who observed that "the Canadian West was opened up, first for furs, then gold, then came beef and finally wheat" ("Ranchers and Ranching," 8 June 1950), who knew the different requirements of black Aberdeen Angus, white-faced Herefords, and square-built red Shorthorns, and who was nuzzled by sheep and dogs in her farm visits, was aware of the fact that her readers were primarily interested in the men and women

PRIZE WHEAT GROWN IN THE FOOTHILLS

By Miriam Green Ellis

1. Tractor and horses are both used by Mr. Wilford in harvesting on the "hill" farm. 2.-Mr. Frelan Wilford. 3. Hogs fit in with wheat farming. 4. Part of the money won at the World's Grain Show went to buy a windmill. 5. The flock of Hampshires thrive on the foothill pasture giving a hundred per cent lamb crop. 6. Mr. and Mrs. Wilford at home.

IT WAS JUST one of those days. No one would believe the sun was umpteen miles away, the heat seemed like the blast from a smelting furnace. Even the hens, cold blooded creatures that they are with their toes or their combs always freezing off, went around feeling sorry for themselves, their wings propped out and their heads drooping pathetically. The pigs dug themselves holes as close to the frost line as possible and even a bucket of mash would not entice them out for a photograph. The old ewes were too hot even to be curious and were only recalled to the present by the bleat of their lambs, which having just been docked, were not too comfortable. Horses hung their heads over the gate, thankful only that most of the spring's work was done.

And the humans?

Air conditioned cars had relieved the pressure coming into Calgary but there was nothing air conditioned about the bus on which the journey continued to Staveley. The engine overheated and refused to function on every hill, and the driver tinkered and fussed and finally took off the hood entirely to give the poor thing as much air as possible, and this at eight o'clock in the

oats a year, the average is around 10,000 to 12,000 bushels. They summerfallowed about one-third of the acreage and the wheat is grown on the fallow land.

After winning the $2,500 prize at Regina, Mr. and Mrs. Wilford sat down and thought and thought about all the ways in which they could use that money. They had driven down to Regina and were camped at the Exhibition camp grounds. What with several repercussions from drouth and grasshoppers there had been a few hard years and the bulk of the money would go to clear up some debts that added nothing to their peace of mind. But one new thing they decided to have before this unexpected windfall disappared from sight entirely. The windfall should finance a windmill, which now stands just at the back door and a pipe carries water to the sheep and pig corrals. Yes, they wanted a new car and several other things, but they could wait, — and did.

Tall and lean and very retiring, Frelan Wilford is just entering his forties, so there is time yet for the new car and the new barns he wants. In the meantime the house is getting a new coat of paint. The house in

field is on the eastern slope, protected well from the west and south west winds that prevail there. It looks more like a range country than a wheat field, and as a matter of fact the summer range for the cattle, sheep and surplus horses lies just above.

It was newly broken land that grew the prize winning sample for Regina, but the Chicago sample last year came from the same corner under the hills and from a crop yielding forty bushels to the acre.

"Is he going to show again this year?" one enquires.

"That depends on the crop," says Wilford, who, retiring to the point of shyness, uses

dropped to fourteen bushels, some third generation Marquis grown under similar conditions averaged only nine bushels.

Last year he grew both the Early Triumph strain of Red Bobs and Reward, the Red Bobs yielding around 25 bushels and Reward 23 bushels, the Reward fields

who farmed, ranched, rode broncos, changed careers, and launched new opportunities. Whether covering pioneer builders like Bishop James Lucas in Aklavik and Reverend George McDougall in Edmonton, or wheat farmers like Joseph Smith of Wolf Creek, near Edson, and Frelan Wilford from the Foothills, who took top prizes as "World's Wheat King" in Chicago and then Regina (18 December 1929; 5 August 1936), or an engineer who became a prosperous seed grower (13 June 1928) and the enterprise that led to a new sugar-beet factory at Picture Butte (7 August 1935), she concentrated on the people who made the story.

Her writing offers acute portraits of people and rituals. Ellis's report of the 1923 Sun Dance at Hobbema conveys the curiosity of a non-participant observer. With "regeneration and thanksgiving" as its major purposes, this communal ceremony, known to the Cree as "nipâhkwêsimowin (Thirst Dance)" (Pettipas

Facing page: "Prize Wheat Grown in the Foothills" *FHWS* 5 August 1936 96-91 MGE 8.I

This page: Photos of Cree Sun Dance at Hobbema, 1923 96-91 MGE 14, VII

Cree Sun Dance at Hobbema, 1923
96-91 MGE 14, VII

57, 56), was a significant milestone. In 1914 an amendment to Section 149 of the Indian Act declared such "indigenous forms of activities ... subject to the approval of the superintendent general of Indian Affairs" (Pettipas 149). Deputy Superintendent General Duncan Scott had given permission for the performance of the Hobbema ceremonies, related very contrastingly in the "sensationalism" (Pettipas 174) of the unattributed account in the *Edmonton Journal*, "Sun Dance of the Crees at Hobbema: By Special Permission of the Government Red Men Observe Wierd [*sic*] Ceremony," and in Ellis's unpublished typescript, "Sun Dance at Hobbema." Member of an invited party of Hudson's Bay Company managers, the *Journal* reporter is ushered into the Sun Dance "hall"; he or she comments on "moist, wet copper bodies," "the flash of white cowrie shells and teeth against dark bodies," and "the inextinguishable crash of the tom-tom" in this "Pagan rite" (3). Taking her own photographs, distinct from those published in the newspaper, Ellis observes from the outside only, yet she captures features of shared human interest.

> For the last Sun Dance five or six hundred Indians had gathered together on an open field at the Hobbema Reserve, their teepees all ranged along two sides and in the central position, the Sun Dance tent which is well worth description. It was large enough to hold between two and three hundred people. ... In the centre was the sacred tree, the trunk of a large poplar placed in the ground and securely braced. This formed as it were the centre pole and to this were attached all the long roof poles.

Cree Sun Dance at Hobbema, 1923 96-91 MGE 14, VII

Comparing the lack of awareness of "the significance of the old pagan ceremonial" among the younger generation to Christian children's loss of "the dramatic significance of Lent, Good Friday and Easter," she admits sadness at witnessing what might be "the last Sun Dance ever to be seen in the West." She marvels at the endurance of the dancers and the intricacy of beaded costumes. She concentrates not on the sweat but on the "ingenuity in the decoration" of the painted faces.

"The cowboy is a species distinct and separate from all the rest of mankind."

The dancers—there were about forty of them, men and women—were decked in their best and their faces were painted in various ways. The medicine man, who, I found, was chiefly responsible for arranging the dance, and one or two others of the men, were naked from the waist up; their bodies were painted a saffron yellow, and decorated in red or blue or green with designs of the moon or horses or possibly just streaks of black across the cheeks. All the dancers had their faces painted in this manner. A few had shown special ingenuity in the decoration. ... The dancers were decorated with all the beads and quill work, feathers and such as go to make up their ceremonial attire. Many of these costumes were as beautiful as any you have seen in the museums, and the weight of this solid bead work is hardly to be conceived without actually having it in one's hand. I could not help but think of this when I watched those men and women after three days of constant dancing.

Toward the end of the ceremony she realizes that some holy importance attends the gentle and reverent handling of the buffalo head behind a drawn screen.

When covering "The Last Great Horse Round-up" (20 August 1930), she trains the spotlight not on a group celebration, but rather on a single figure, the cowboy himself, offering this character sketch:

The cowboy is a species distinct and separate from all the rest of mankind. He rides as though moulded to his horse; he is friend to his horse, but also his master. Many a day, and night too, they spend together on the open range. The rider sleeps with his saddle for a pillow while his horse grazes not far away. Should danger threaten, the faithful beast gives the signal.

You can always tell a cowboy, they say, for he puts on his hat first, then his boots and his pants, while a city man just reverses the process. But the city man does not have to put his foot down on the cold floor of a shack.

At the E.P. (Edward, Prince of Wales) Ranch, in Pekisko, near High River, MGE turns her attention to the animals, noting how the "stock from the Old Country," including Shorthorn cattle, Dartmoor ponies, Shropshire sheep, and Clydesdale horses, have been bred and sold to several ranches in

Facing page: Final Ceremony at Cree Sun Dance, Hobbema
96-91 MGE 14.VII

California, particularly the Los Robles and Annandel herds at Santa Rosa ("Alberta Ranch, A Link of Empire").

Sharp contrasts between periods of boom and desiccation comprise her accounts of the drought of the thirties. When, in 1931, "a pittance of three inches of rain has fallen at Regina during the present crop season," she reports on the thriving growth of western bull thistle and the winds that have blown surface soil "right down to hardpan"; she observes on the journey from Regina to Swift Current, "where ordinarily there would be scores of threshing machines and combines in early September, I saw two and they had spit out a pathetic little mound of straw about as big as a table" ("The Tragedy of the Regina Plains," 30 September 1931). But the subsequent plans for rural rehabilitation, jointly shared by federal, provincial, and municipal governments, prompt more optimistic reports of the move back to the land. In "Men on Relief Go Back to Land" (7 June 1933), she records that farmers who had moved to the city are now returning, "and mostly the children are moving with them." As she explains, always spinning a narrative, "Maybe the boy got married while they were in the city, and in the staff

Family Herald and Weekly Star, September 30, 1936 — Three

ALBERTA RANCH, A LINK OF EMPIRE

By Miriam Green Ellis

1. Gateway to the E. P. Ranch with letters "E." "P.," one on each pillar. 2. Ranch house as seen from the north east. 3. W. L. Carlyle, manager of the Ranch. 4. Hampshires in pleasant surroundings. 5. Princeton Nerissa and calf. 6. Princeton Paragon by Bapton. 7. Princeton on Guard.

RUMORS about the disposal of the E. P. Ranch at Pekisko, Alberta, come as thick and fast as the rumors about the supposed marriage of the owner of that ranch. The gentleman owner of this ranch takes his kingly prerogative of holding his own counsel. It was announced soon after his accession to the throne that according to rule and precedent and all the rest, the King could own no property outside Great Britain, but the new King, no doubt, takes it that he is also King of Canada and so could easily invent a new precedent if he so wished.

There have been rumors that he had offered it to the Government of Canada to add to their Experimental Farm system, and latterly that he had offered it to the Fairview Home for English Boys which has a farm on Vancouver Island. He might possibly wish to keep it, especially if he carries on with the other rumor of visiting his Dominions, for there is little doubt that he found wonderful relaxation in his little ranch home in the Foothills of Alberta. There he put on old clothes, and helped with all the farm work that happened to be doing around the place from "mucking out the byre" to pitching off sheaves. And at night he came back to the quiet fireplace and talked about the future of the ranch as any other ranch owner might.

Apart from a Canadian retreat for himself when he might happen to be passing this way, the then Prince of Wales had in mind a stock improvement ranch in Canada similar to the nobility places in the Old Country, where good foundation stock could be bred and sold to the farmers. When W. L. Carlyle, who was put in as manager of the ranch, suggested holding some of the stock to build up a herd there, the Prince's reply was that if anyone wanted to buy them, to sell, as the E. P. could always get more from the big herds in the Old Country.

They have Clydesdale horses, Shorthorn cattle, Hampshire sheep, but no pigs. There are Dartmoor ponies on the range and an Arab stallion. The manager does not like pigs on the hoof, but takes his breakfast bacon as regularly as any other. The stock has been exhibited at the larger fairs as attested by drawers full of medals and ribbons.

The stolid Chinese cook brings forth from his refrigerator a cut of beef and out of his garden some vegetables so that all visitors have good ranch fare. The refrigerator is large enough to put away a side of beef and a few pieces of lamb besides. In the living room are pictures of the late King Edward with some of his favorite horses. One shows him with "Persimmon" by St. Simon out of Perditta which won the Epsom in 1896. The visitors' book is an interesting item in itself for it is as cosmopolitan as is Canada, and the names therein range all the way from that of the Royal owner to the cowboys next door.

It was the will of the Prince to keep this place, just such a ranch home as any progressive rancher might have and for some time it remained as it was when bought. But when the Prince came through with a considerable retinue, Manager Carlyle had to build on an addition, and this was done with the idea of holding the original ranch house idea as much as possible. He gathered stones for the new fireplace from here and there, and each bit of glacial rock has a history in itself. A stone club, handled by dear knows what old Indian chief, centres the fireplace masonry. Presents are not accepted at the E. P., but there are one or two. The lights beside the fire place have large German shells for their base. There are fur rugs on the floor and a few Oriental and one hooked rug made by the Habitant women of Quebec, in commemoration of the Diamond jubilee; the pattern on this rug is the British Coat of Arms. The fireplace lamps and the hooked rug are gifts to the E.P. There is also another rug made by the British Columbia Indians, in their own distinctive designs.

The long porch across the west side of the living room faces the Rockies. Sometimes these mountains are yellow, sometimes soft pastel shades, but the morning that I sat and looked across the rolling hills toward the higher peaks, they were deep blue.

There has never been any doubt that the Prince's interest in the E. P. Ranch was very genuine. It was to be his Canadian home and he has been loth to change it in any way from its former identity. The pedigrees for the animals still come in the name of the Prince of Wales, and the trophy which he annually presents for the championship for the Canadian bucking horse riding at the Calgary stampede was presented again this year as the Edward Prince of Wales trophy, although technically speaking there is no Prince of Wales now.

Aldebaran, the Arab stallion, is sixteen years old now, but has all the pep and action of a colt. One might as well try to take a picture of a humming bird. The dam of this horse came from Arabia, one of the very few mares which the Arabs have ever allowed to leave their home shores.

He is rather small for his kind but beautifully formed and typically Arabian. For six years he has been crossed on the Dartmoor ponies, making a very desirable small sized saddle horse. For one year he stood at Provost, Alberta, where he was bred to saddle mares and half breeds. There is also a Dartmoor stallion, Teign Gate, which came from the moors beside the River Teign. He is the sire or the grandsire of every pony on the place. Ten or eleven Dartmoor pony mares are bred each year, which is about all the trade will take. High class ponies for children have been luxuries that have been cut down during the past few years, but there are still some orders coming from as far East as Toronto. For instance, a telegram: "Send me another Dartmoor pony same as one bought at Edmonton last year."

The Clydesdales have won their spurs at the different shows and about six or seven colts are raised each year. Clydesdales have entirely replaced the Percherons formerly kept at the ranch.

Breeding animals that have gone farthest and widest over the continent are the Shorthorn cattle. Among the families that have done best in this herd are the Mars Goldies and the Wimples. Princeton Neptune that went to California last year at $2,000 was of Wimple breeding. Mr. Carlyle considers Shylock one of the best breeding bulls they have had on the place. Two years ago his get was first in a string of thirteen groups at Chicago and second the same year at the Toronto Royal. King of the Fairies, later sold to the States, was a good

(Continued on Next Page.)

Left: "Alberta Ranch Link of Empire"
FHWS 30 September 1936 96-91 MGE 8.1

curtailments of the last few years, he now finds himself out of a job, so he takes his wife back to the home farm so they can all work together for a living, and the old mother has the job of teaching the city girl how to keep house on a farm." Interviewing both husband and wife about the return to the land is essential. In the opinion of the interviewing committee, "the wife's suitability and willingness is quite as important as the husband's." MGE includes a telling anecdote about a woman criticized for her resistance to going to the country with her husband: "But it turned out that the nice kind husband that was anxious to go to the country was out on suspended sentence for wife beating."

Spectacular differences in terrain can account for a successful livelihood in an area associated with drought. "A Land Where Dinosaurs Roamed" (26 August 1936) relates the story of a farm "situated at the edge of the dinosaur bones which have been collected by all the best museums in the country." Well in advance of the establishment of the Royal Tyrrell Museum of Palaeontology, MGE comments on two vistas: "The bed and banks of the Red Deer at this point are eerie,

Right: "A Land Where Dinosaurs Roamed"
FHWS 26 August 1936 96-91 MGE 8.1

A LAND WHERE DINOSAURS ROAMED

By Miriam Green Ellis

1. Yorkshire sows qualified in Advanced Registry, on farm of P. J. Rock, Morrin, Alberta. 2. Farm buildings and ground sloping to dam. 3. Range cattle, a minor feature of Mr. Rock's farm. 4. Hampshire sheep. 5. Mrs. P. J. Rock and daughter, Margery.

FOR YEARS, the name of P. J. Rock, Morrin, has been attached to various prize winning samples of grain at seed shows all over the continent. I have seen him attending directors' meetings of the Canadian Seed Growers and the provincial seed growers, but this year when I found him director in charge of the swine at the Calgary Exhibition, I felt that an investigation should be made. All the Royal Commissions seemed to be busy investigating coal and wheat and rayons and the like, so I undertook to do this one myself at the usual per diem.

In the first place I found that the initials P. J. really stand for something. Everyone seemed to call him P. J. and I thought it was one of those cases where parents had not taken the responsibility of giving a name, but had just set up a pair of initials and let him choose a name after, which of course he had never done. But his wife does not call him P. J. and from her I learned that P. J. really stands for Philip John. She calls her husband John and her son Philip, so both names are in use around the home where the Rocks farm some 3,000 acres.

It is no little series of demonstration plots from which P. J. draws his samples for the seed shows, and I may as well say at the beginning that there was ample reason for his being director of the swine ring at Calgary too. His pigs are real ones, three of the sows being qualified in advanced registry. One of his boars sold at at the Calgary sale last fall. So that was that.

Originally Devonshire people, the Rocks came to this country in 1906 on their wedding trip. Previous to that, however, P. J. had been looking after his father's farm in Suffolk for some twelve years, where he had been chiefly occupied in raising malting barley and shipping the milk from forty head of cows to the London market. The fathers and uncles and the grandfathers before them had been farmers in the Old Country, so there was nothing in the mind of P. J. when he came to this country but to farm.

****

Recalling those days in the Old Country, Mr. Rock tells of cutting all the barley with a scythe. They stopped cutting at nine in the morning, had a glass of beer, and cocked and stacked that same afternoon. It was necessary to hold the color in order to make the pale ale.

They came to Calgary in 1906 and after riding around the country with his wife's brothers, the Grenvilles, who are also years later they all took up their preemptions.

But in the meantime, this canny Englishman had rented a farm near Calgary, kept cows and sold the milk in town, put up hay and in such manner, kept the family going till three years later they moved out to the new location at Morrin, northeast of Calgary. That was before the Goose Lake line was built, and their nearest station was Acme, forty-two miles away. They considered that too far to haul wheat, so unless they were going to town anyway, they did not bother to take wheat till they had a station at Munson.

Since then they have added the odd quarter section to the original holdings and they have learned a lot about Canadian farming that they or their grandfathers had not known with all their experience of Old Country farming. For instance, they had not known about smut, but since 1914 P. J. has never failed to treat his seed, and it has paid well.

With some 2,300 acres under cultivation, the Rocks summerfallow half of it every year, which is none too good considing that every bit of land is growing registered or certified seed. Marquis is their big crop and they grow their own elite stock, make their own selections. The Elite gives an average return of around 40 bushels to the acre. They also grow Reward, Victory and Legacy oats, Trebi barley, and a little O.A.C. barley. There is also some flax for the stock, some crested wheat grass, brome and sweet clover. There is a supply of feed and forage crops, for they have always kept stock around the place, and now there are a few pure bred Shorthorns coming on, as well as the Yorkshire pigs and Hampshire sheep.

"Although there have been some dry years, we have never had a complete failure here," said Mr. Rock, "but some years we had to get a few seed oats. The lowest crop we ever had was ten years ago when it ran eight bushels to the acre.

"We always had a few cattle on the place," he adds, "and in 1928 I saw the drought coming and so got the hogs and sheep."

There are sixty pure bred Hampshire ewes, which with the young stock makes 150 to 160 sheep to winter. The Yorkshires, mostly of Lacombe Experimental Farm breeding, are all on advanced registry, which is a step away from the homestead days when they put up salt pork for the family larder.

On a seed farm, much care has to be taken in keeping the different varieties separate, but on a three thousand acre out-

the wide single disk and the rod weeder. It is a bad country for the pale Western cutworm, but by not working the summerfallows from August 1 to the middle of September, the Rocks have eliminated this pest absolutely. Brome discourages the sawfly, which is also bad in this country.

The Reward wheat is combined, the Marquis is cut with the binder, but cut high enough that there is good stubble.

The straw scatterer is run behind the combine, to spread the straw, One section has a bad habit of drifting if given half a chance, and on this place practically no ploughing has been done since 1925 and sixteen rod strips are now being used to check the tendency to blow.

They have to go down 175 to 250 feet for water, but the original stock watering dam near the house is still there and still in use. The sheep pasturing on ten-acre strips of crested grass have open access to this water hole. As a matter of fact the sheep pastured only one end of these crested wheat grass fields; the other end was coming on for a seed crop.

Wheat as a feed is not taboo on the Rock farm. In fact everything but the milk cows get wheat; even the horses take it and like it. But the straw and sweet clover and whatever else is available at the time all goes through the hammer mill and is fed to the cows. And the cows on this farm have to give milk.

"We do not keep a cow that will not give 9,000 pounds of milk. We want the surplus milk for the pigs," says Mr. Rock.

****

So in spite of fighting drought since 1928, there has been a livelihood at this farm situated at the edge of the dinosaur bones which have been collected by all the best museums in the country. The Red Deer River with its queer formations runs alongside this farm, and it was son Philip's favorite occupation before he started to Agricultural College to climb to the most dangerous tip of some of these hoodoos and scare his parents to death. Possibly he was looking for swallows' nests, possibly just looking. The bed and banks of the Red Deer at this point are eerie and give a queer feeling, especially if it is just at that time between sun down and dark, but the farms just up beyond are pastoral in the extreme. The vegetation of that almost prehistoric time that produced dinosaurs has also been preserved in the coal fields that abound in that country. Winter fuel is no problem for the Drumheller-Morrin country.

tered seed in this country?" was the natural question.

It seems that back as far as 1915 the Munson Agricultural Society came into existence; out of that in 1924 the Morrin Seed Growers' Society was started with the purpose of improving the seed. The membership to that has been as high as fifty-six and ever since its inception P. J. Rock has been president and A. C. B. Grenville the secretary. Fields crops competitions came into existence and the interest in pure seed increased instantly.

For several years the Brooks district held the International Harvester shield for high points won by a community at the provincial seed fairs, but the Morrin Society finally pushed them from this pedestal and held the honor for some six or seven years. Then Lethbridge stepped up, but not for a moment must it be thought that Morrin is going to keep looking up at Lethbridge for any considerable time.

"Have you ever been back to England?" I asked Mr. Rock.

"No," he admitted, "we planned to go several times, but just then a quarter section we wanted seemed always to come on the market, and we took the passage money to make a down payment. No, we never got back."

But in the meantime the eighty-year-old Sussex father has come out and a brother, Stanley. The father seems as happy on the Canadian farm as though he were in his Sussex garden, and Stanley appears to bear considerable authority around the stock barns. So three generations of Rocks are adding their quota to Canadian life and citizenship. It is tempting to make a pun about the English Rocks and the dinosaurs but we will refrain.

PLANTS TAINT MILK.

Much has been done to eliminate barn flavors in milk, but so far little attention has been paid to plants that taint milk, giving it an unpleasant flavor or odor. Certain taints undoubtedly arise from plants eaten in the pasture or hay, and steps should be taken to eradicate them when they occur in abundance. Fortunately not every highly flavored or perfumed plant eaten will taint the milk. The noxious product must be digested by the cow if it is to go into the milk. The commonest taint is onion which comes from the cow eating wild leeks or onions. Buttercups will cause bitterness if eaten in quantity when green, though in the dried state in hay they are harmless. Oxeye daisies, chamomile, tansey

especially if it is just at that time between sun down and dark, but the farms just up beyond are pastoral in the extreme."

Government plans to encourage livestock production where wheat farming had failed, under the Prairie Farm Rehabilitation Act, are an opportunity for MGE to address the issue of overproduction and the stubbornness of a few farmers. "Land Once in Wheat Goes Back to Cattle" (20 October 1943) delineates "the lure of wheat" in boom times: "So the prairie wool was turned under and the cattle line was pushed back. Wheat was planted and grew and sold at high prices, encouraging more people to move in, break sod, and grow wheat." With the bad years, she relates, "hundreds of thousands of acres were abandoned, with only the odd farmer staying on in a dust-banked house—staying because he hadn't the energy or the means to move out, or because his faith in the land was absolutely unshakeable."

Among the innovations in the offing, of which MGE may not have been entirely aware when she

Family Herald and Weekly Star, September 24. 1941

Students are here seen sketching the Bow River Falls, with the Banff Springs Hotel and Sulphur Mountain in the background. Right: Mrs. Mary Meigs Atwater, Basin, Montana, president of the American Shuttlecraft Guild, instructs Mrs. Edward Anthony, New York City, in an old Egyptian mode of weaving, done by turning the cards. Below: A weaving class in action.

Banff Fine Arts School

By Miriam Green Ellis

FROM the four corners of the continent they come to the School of Fine Arts at Banff. Among these students there is contrast in superlative degree and at the same time a ridiculous similarity. Some stay for the month at the palatial Banff Springs Hotel; others at the camp grounds down by the Bow River; there are farm folks and West enders; there are Indians and whites; Southern accents and English evacuees; they come from California and Quebec; from Vancouver Island, Alabama and Florida. But there is a common denominator for them all, their love of the arts and their desire to learn more. Rich and poor sit together on a rock or a campstool to sketch the Bow Falls or the mountain tops; they fraternize at the drama lectures and help each other choose colors for weaving or pottery, or to find an idle piano for practising.

Organized by the University of Alberta eight or nine years ago, it is still a new project, but its rapid development indicates that its con-

getting such materials as felspar. The clays come from Medicine Hat. The weaving has proved particularly popular, due partly to the general interest in handicrafts and mostly to the fact that Mary Meigs Atwater, Basin, Montana, is the instructor. Mrs. Meigs is head of the American Shuttlecraft Guild and dean of American hand weavers. J. B. McLellan, graduate of the Glasgow School of Art, and now on the staff of the Provincial Institute of Technology and Art, Calgary, teaches the modelling and pottery.

Jacques Jolas, director of Music Extension at Cornell College, Iowa, is back for the fourth year. Professor Albert L. Cru, head of the French department at Teacher's College, Columbia University, heads up the French section and is assisted by Yvonne L. Poirier, also of New York.

There is also a library division, a co-operative arrangement between the Extension branch of the University of Alberta and McGill Library School. It is under the ... of G. R. Lomer of McGill,

teachers' certificates by all the departments of education right across Canada.

Learning to parley vous, or pot or paint at Banff, is surely getting education in its most liquid and attractive form. As a locale for a school of fine arts, Banff is just a "natural". It has everything from sky high mountains to complacent bears down by the rubbish piles, rainbows that prop themselves up on spruce trees and property Indians in full feathers that hang around the C. P. R. Hotel, willing to have their pictures taken as so much per; hordes of tourists that come on railroad trains, buses, Lincolns, jalopies, airplanes or bicycles built for two; there is just room along the river bank for one of the most beautiful golf courses in the world, and if one must get serious there are the hot health-giving sulphur springs that bubble up from some uneasy spot in the earth's anatomy that has grown weary of holding a mountain on its stomach. There is scenery plus at Banff; indeed, half a dozen of Canada's leading artists have established homes there.

Small wonder that folk come from all over the continent to attend the Fine Arts School at Banff. The first year it was in existence, most of the students came from Alberta; now more than half come from outside the province.

the best essay on "What does the High School dramatic society contribute to the community?"; the other two awarded for the best one-act play. In Saskatchewan through the department of Extension of the University and the Provincial

Drama Leag[...]
are given in t[...]
stipulated tha[...]
must be from[...]
were won by[...]
Waseca: M[...]

(Turn to

Banff Fine Arts School

completed [...]
Cravens ha[...]
side, bringi[...]
to attend t[...]
painting an[...]
to see good[...]

Henry House, MGE, Henry George Glyde at Athabasca Glacier, Columbia Icefield, 1941
(courtesy Glenbow Archives NA 5660-20)

reported on the use of the oil sands for superior and durable surfaces of roads in "Asphalt From North for Road Paving" (13 April 1932), was the ongoing research of Dr. Karl Clark of the Scientific and Industrial Research Council of Alberta, who had already established a pilot plant at Clearwater to investigate ways of making the bituminous sands of greater value to the province. However, she must have had more than an inkling of potential wealth when in "Down North" she referred to Fort McMurray as possibly "a second Klondyke." The boom-town atmosphere of Edmonton, with the influx of American engineers during the building of the Alaska Highway, in "Booming City Greets Show" (21 April 1943), results in some full-throated boosterism: "even at 40 or 50 below the buildings proceeded to rise up and hammers pounded, and huge aircraft landed for fuel or repairs and went on mysteriously into the night." A similar excited energy is discernible in her coverage of the fledgling and popular arts school, "Banff Fine Arts School," a celebration of "education in its most liquid and attractive form," underscored with MGE's firm belief in "aesthetic values" enriching a diversity of communities. She is also full of pride about the enormous success of the Stampede: "Calgary Goes on Stampede—Records fall all over the place as Calgary stages what is probably the greatest stampede in history" (25 July 1945).

"Stampede Millinery"
FHWS 2 September 1942
96-91 MGE 8.II

Family Herald and Weekly Star, September 2, 1942

Stampede Millinery

Masculine headgear at Calgary Stampede so thrills Miriam Green Ellis that she snaps a dozen different varieties

By R. S. Kennedy

MIRIAM GREEN ELLIS is such a dyed in the wool Westerner that the Calgary stampede is always inclined to go to her head. This year it did so with the startling result that she devoted quite unexpected attention to hats.

Here therefore, we have a dozen pictures of millinery models snapped at the Calgary stampede,—but no story!

Instead of the usual packed typewritten pages of winners of Junior, Senior and Grand Champions, the vivid word pictures of the blaze of a big exhibition which accompany the typical Ellis exhibition story, we have just a string of hats and no story at all.

It is true that Miriam Green Ellis has deigned to identify some of the heads under the hats, but we have it in her own writing that this selection was sent along "in case somebody could write an article about hats." And while she identified most of the heads, she did not identify the hats,—which, as any woman ought to know are much more important.

While we have done our best to fill the gap and ourselves write a learned, and at the same time, fully "fashion conscious" story on this display of male millinery, we suggest that readers consult an encyclopedia or astrologer before they bet any money on the accuracy of our comments.

Luckily there is a little thoroughly reliable information available on the Stetson hat which may be considered the trade mark of the Westerner and which is the ancestor of many of the samples shown here. John B. Stetson, son of a Philadelphia hatter, who had gone west to seek a cure for tuberculosis, is said to have made the first of them; just to suit his special needs. He made the felt from fur and rabbit skins with the aid of a hatchet and improvised tools. He wore it constantly and it became so admired that a cowboy gave him $5 for it.

When he got back to Philadelphia, cured, he made a number of sample hats which he entitled "The Boss of the Plains," and sent them out to Western dealers. These hats caught on like wild fire. They were handy for fanning camp fires, for blindfolding horses, for slapping steers, for fighting grass fires, replacing broken windowpanes, and for targets for the old six shooter.

When he died at the age of 76, in 1906, John B. Stetson was making hundreds of thousands of hats each year. The West has changed, ranching has changed, but the Ten Gallon Stetson has only changed by splitting up into an infinite variety of models.

However, long before the Stetson became the trade mark of the plains, the Indians had developed their own millinery in a far more spectacular way. So we will start off our description by introducing, at the top left-hand corner of this page, a model which we have christened the EARLY SCALPING BONNET, displayed by "One Spot," a young, and apparently rather coy Indian from the Sarcee Reserve. This is about the most chic line of millinery ever created in Canada, and the only one in which Canada is the style centre instead of Paris or New York.

Third along the top row come two millinery styles which are growing more popular every day, whether in Calgary, New York or the Yukon. The Canadian boy is wearing the AERIAL BEAVER, and the Yank is wearing the EAGLE EGG. The former is worn tilted over the right ear, and the latter over the left,—just to show that there still is an invisible line which separates, but does not divide them.

Two Stetson creations fill up the top row. On the right smiling Eddie Burton of Claresholm, Alta., who brought his Highland steers to the Stampede, models the TEN GALLON WHITE DE LUXE. This hat is a very swanky little item, of the great Stetson racial group.

Dave Day of Bowness Park, has the other member of the family in the top row—though only a poor relation of it,—the TEN GALLON WRITISH DE CAYED. These two hats exemplify the principle which your wife has undoubtedly emphasized to you, that the kind of hats women wear has a great effect on their internal poise and confidence. Thus Eddie Burton wears the typical, confident smile of the DE LUXE owner while owners of the DE CAYED variety have that suspicious and sombre expression with which Dave Day regards the camera.

From Grandma's girlhood days women's hats have held the limelight. Each spring mere men have held their breath until the Easter parade has shown what new monstrosities have been perpetrated. Leghorns, picture hats, pillboxes, sailors, crownless, brimless, bevelled or beburnoosed, have been the subject of bitter controversy throughout the years.

While women's crowns have thus been shamelessly publicized men's headpieces have been brutally ignored. It has been claimed that they're not interesting enough to bother about. On this page we present graphic evidence of the falsity of this opinion. And it is indeed fitting that this belated recognition of male millinery should come from the lens of a woman, and that this woman should be Miriam Green Ellis, one of whose many claims to fame is her own hatlessness.

Varied Designs

Coming down the left-hand column, we start with Frank Stamford, cashier and accountant with the Calgary Exhibition for 22 years, who models the FINANCIAL PANAMA, a smart item designed for business men who are Liberal enough to recognize that seasons change, but who are too Conservative to sacrifice style to perspiration, and who have plenty of Social Credit at the bank.

The hat below is at the extreme opposite scale in the hat hierarchy and is known as the DIXIE HOSS HAT. It is being modelled by an unknown gentleman from Dixie, who follows the horses, not only as a means of livelihood but as a satisfying spiritual experience,—as shown by his expression. This hat fulfills the fundamental function of a hat by covering the upper portion of the head, but in addition, it can be used for wiping off sweat, polishing boots and other non-functional but useful jobs.

Next Tommy Campbell, from Londonderry in Northern Ireland, displays the TORPEDO TURBAN, one of the Royal Canadian Navy's smartest summer models, which is attracting growing attention in Nazi yachting circles.

At the bottom of the column is the STETSON WEEK-DAY BLACK, shown by Doff Aber, of Wolf, Wyoming. It is particularly suitable for every day practical work and funerals, as it does not show the dirt or have to be dyed. It is said to have been developed from the original Stetson in those earlier and wilder western days, when it was more difficult to separate funerals from week-day work than at present and when the only convenient way to get a hat cleaned was not to have it show the dirt.

At the top of the right-hand column is the famous GLENGARRY MUNICIPAL BONNET, containing Major Andrew Davidson, perennial Mayor of Calgary, and Alberta M.P.P. This model is a consistent vote-getter and its compact streamlines are invaluable when leaning over to kiss babies.

A Working Model

The washable model of the STALIN TOQUE which follows is Herdsman Bill Fraser's effort to show a solid farm-labor front for Coaldale. It is an expansible as well as a washable model, and popular with herdsmen who expect to win grand championships, and do not want to split their hat bands!

The next model, worn by Eneas McCormack, Calgary merchant and director of the Exhibition, is by the same modiste as the STETSON WEEK-DAY BLACK shown at the bottom of the other column. This is the STETSON SUNDAY PURPLE. It is not used for work but can be worn at exceptionally interesting, important or Royal funerals, or when shooting up a church. It is seen at its best when wrapped in cellophane, which may be tied with purple ribbon.

The last one is the STETSON TEN GALLON SQUASH. It is a special model for Managers and Millionaires, who want an extremely costly item which can nevertheless be worn with the same lofty disregard of style as the DIXIE HOSS HAT, and which will not blow off when the shareholders blow up! It is being modelled here by J. Charles Yule, Manager of the Calgary Stampede. The wide, gently curved brim corrects the discrepancy between the chest line and the waist line, which is so frequent in millionaires and managers, and also serves to emphasize the rounded curve of the shoulders caused by patiently bearing great responsibilities, and by long hours of stooping over a desk or a poker table.

west of Wetaskiwin, Alber
Campbell, Edmonton;
Forbes, Drumheller; Mr
Lambert, Lethbridge;
Robinson, Morley, were all
ship winners in art.
There were three o
Britishers evacuated to th

"Banff Fine Arts School" *FHWS*, 21 April 1943 96-91 MGE 8.II

Miriam Green Ellis

Why Miriam Matters

THIS EXHIBIT'S SELECTIVE SAMPLING of the wealth in the MGE Collection is an invitation to others to explore its treasures. As a reflection of an engaged, creative life, the Collection's "archivization" is not a type of "imprisonment" (Scott 143), but rather an informed opening to an era whose influences can still be felt. The archive of a past that the Collection contains evidences both the donor's precise organization of contents and her willingness to include everything, that is, "selected and consciously chosen documentation ... and mad fragments that just ended up there" (Steedman 68).

When Miriam editorializes about her territory of over two thousand miles in "Out West with the Weekly" (October 1951), she stoutly maintains that agricultural reporting "means covering the most important industry ... even in Alberta where oil, gas, coal, minerals make headlines." "It takes seven league boots," she argues with a typical flourish, "to cover the western parish from the Head of the Lakes to Vancouver Island." When talking with farmers and ranchers, two "entirely different breed[s] of cats," the reporter, she acknowledges, "has to be nimble enough to hop from a conversation about round-ups to new combines without letting on that he has ever heard tell of the other." Nimbleness in Miriam's case also involves keeping "track of what is doing at the agricultural colleges and experimental farms, check[ing] on the crops, on new varieties of disease-resistant grains." The fact that she single-handedly ran the western editorial office of the *Family Herald and Weekly Star* and took all the photographs for her own copy—"thousands" of them—illustrates the all-round competence of the woman who was capturing a sense of the West for generations of readers.

The wistfulness of her Memory Book entry "But—," following her account of the retirement dinner festivities, hints that she did not go gentle into that good night.

Facing page:
Portrait of MGE, 1956
96-91 MGE 2.X.11

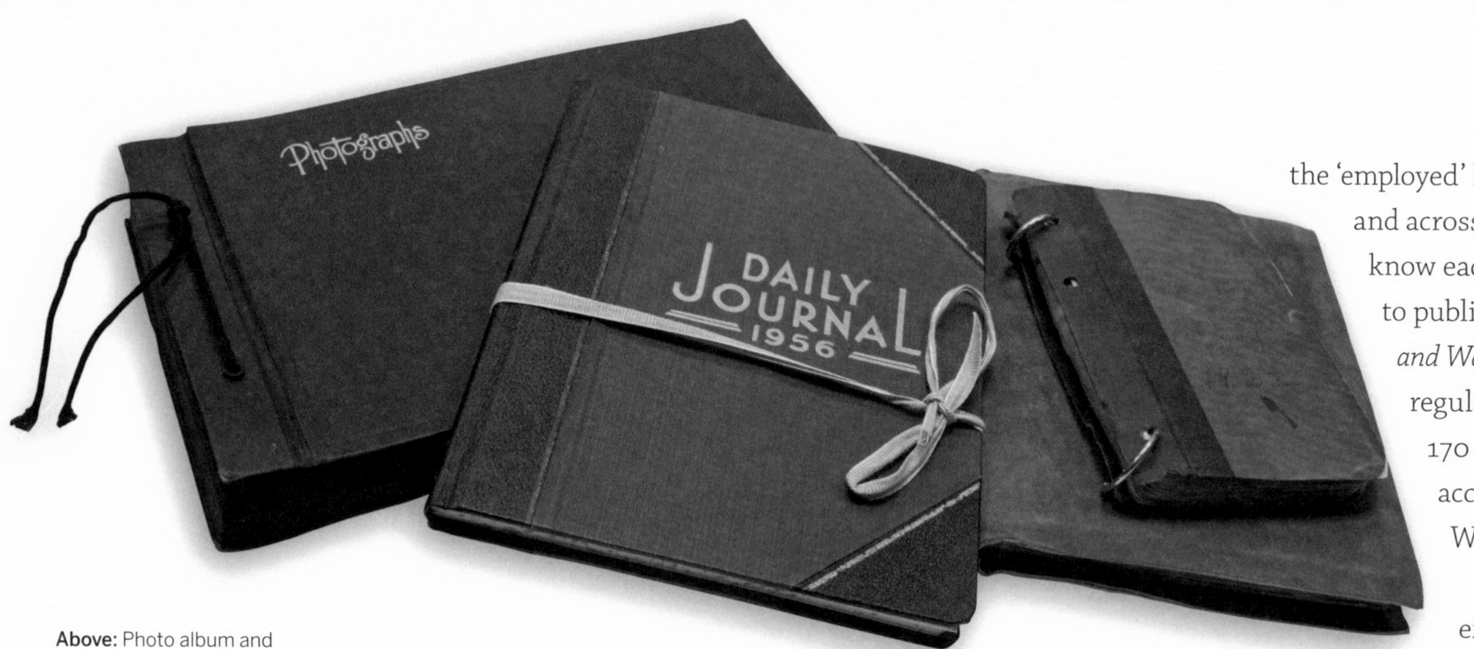

Above: Photo album and typed diary of Aklavik trip along with Memory Book and Daily Journal

Facing page: "Memory Book" opening 96-91 MGE 1.1

Although Miriam did not rave, burn, or rage, she likely nursed the sense that, after decades of pioneering journalism, she still had much more to offer. It is this concept of underused capacity that informs her post-retirement article "Veterans Don't Fade" (15 July 1954), with its observation about "what a lot of agricultural experience and knowledge is being shoved over the edge." The roster of retired agricultural officials she includes is entirely masculine, yet she might have been pondering her own situation as she remarked, "When they were on the 'employed' list they moved around and across Canada, and we all got to know each other." She continued to publish in the *Family Herald and Weekly Star*, but not with the regularity (in 1943 she logged 170 contributions) or assured acceptance of her time as Western Editor.

The friendships Miriam experienced within the Canadian Women's Press Club, with its aims "to improve and maintain the status of journalism as a profession for women and to provide counsel and promote understanding and assistance among press women" ("Constitution," 1), were another form of sustaining community. She lived through the CWPC's transitional stage, as Marjory Lang charts the post-World War II era, when coy nicknames like "paper dolls and newsies" (Lang 285) became acceptable. These were categories in which Miriam definitely did not fit. While her career enlarges the scope of the pioneer

July 21 - Larry met me and on to Saskatoon per Hydramatic via Lockwood and Lake Manitou. Too crowded to swim.

July 22 - St Peters College Father Leonard.

Had to use force to make Jack allow me to drive my own car.

July 26 - Round Lake

July 29 - Hunt - Shroeder

Aug 3 - Met Jean - Round Lake.

Aug 24 Lac La Ronge
Angus Mackinnon Campbell.

Aug 26. Melfort, Tisdale White Fox, Nipawin J. D. MacFarlane

Aug 28-29. For J. G. Gardiner at Lemberg. He has a nice farm and knows what it is all about. Had dinner with the Gardiners.

Coming back to Brandon next day, passed several truck loads of horses. Apparently there is a big market in the States.

Spent the rest of the week at Minnedosa getting an "average small town" story.

It is a lovely harvest season.

journalists Janice Fiamengo studies, Agnes Maule Machar (1837–1927), Sara Jeanette Duncan (1861–1922), Pauline Johnson (1861–1913), Kathleen Blake Coleman (1856–1915), Flora MacDonald Denison (1867–1913), and Nellie McClung (1873–1951), Miriam's work also supplies an opportunity to fulfil Fiamengo's charges to future criticism: to attend "to details of language and ... the manifold relationships between writers, texts, and their audiences" (Fiamengo 216).

The example of Miriam Green Ellis does encourage us to think more broadly about writing. Embedded in quotidian realities, imbued with a strong personality, prepared for a deadline and often illustrated with photographs, necessarily conscious of readers' expectations yet daring to embark for territory not typically considered women's realm, Miriam's writing invites us to consider

"Before the Battle" and "When Nellie Came Back" at Lacombe airfield, 1920 [photo album] 96-91 MGE 1.II

the fundamental elements of viewpoint, narrative line, and emotional response. In the pre-digital age of journalism, she becomes her own search engine, cataloguer, and illustrator—always willing to embrace the "adventure of the unexpected." While vestiges of her world remain and other aspects have eclipsed her expectations, Miriam's writing continues to offer a window on where we have come from. Her independence, boldness, and unshakeable loyalties also crystallize the spirit of the West she so vividly prized. *

"Everbody Talks" [photo album] 96-91 MGE 1.II (left to right: Jack McClung, Nellie McClung, MGE and Wop May at the McClung home)

Works Cited

Aberdeen, Marchioness of Aberdeen [Ishbel Gordon]. *Through Canada with a Kodak*. Introduction Marjory Harper. Toronto: University of Toronto Press, 1994.

Cameron, Agnes Deans. *The New North; Being Some Account of a Woman's Journey through Canada to the Arctic.* New York: D. Appleton and Company, 1910.

"Constitution, Canadian Women's Press Club." Provincial Archives of Alberta, PA. 74. 56/6.

Cram, J.S. "Retiring Editor Honored." *Family Herald and Weekly Star* 15 January 1953, 7+

Dufferin, Marchioness of Dufferin and Ava. *My Canadian Journal, 1872–78; Extracts from My Letters Home While Lord Dufferin was Governor-General.* New York: D. Appleton and Co., 1891.

Ellis, George E. "Annual Report of Edmonton Inspector of Schools," in *Annual Report of the Department of Education of the Province of Alberta, 1906*. Edmonton: Jas. E. Richards, Government Printer, 1907, 54–56.

Ellis, Miriam Green. "Alberta Ranch, A Link of Empire." *Family Herald and Weekly Star,* 30 September 1936. MGE Collection, Bruce Peel Special Collections Library, Box 8, folder I.

———. "A Land Where Dinosaurs Roamed." *Family Herald and Weekly Star,* 26 August 1936. MGE Collection, BPSC, Box 8, folder I.

———. "Alone." ts, MGE Collection, BPSC, Box 2, folder III.

———. "Asphalt From North For Road Paving." *Family Herald and Weekly Star,* 13 April 1932. MGE Collection, BPSC, Box 11, folder I.

———. "A War Bride's Return." ts and ms, MGE Collection, BPSC, Box 2, folder IV.

———. "Banff Fine Arts School." *Family Herald and Weekly Star,* 24 September 1941. MGE Collection, BPSC, Box 8, folder II.

———. "Booming City Greets Show." *Family Herald and Weekly Star,* 21 April 1943. MGE Collection, BPSC, Box 8, folder II.

———. "Canada Has Something." Rotary Ladies' Night, Yorkton, Saskatchewan. MGE Collection, BPSC, Box 12, folder VIII.

———. "Diary of Trip to Midnight Sun." MGE Collection, BPSC, Box 3, folder I.

———. "Down North." ts, MGE Collection, BPSC, Box 3, folder II.

———. "Engineer Becomes Seed Grower." *Family Herald and Weekly Star,* 13 June 1928. MGE Collection, BPSC, Box 8, folder I.

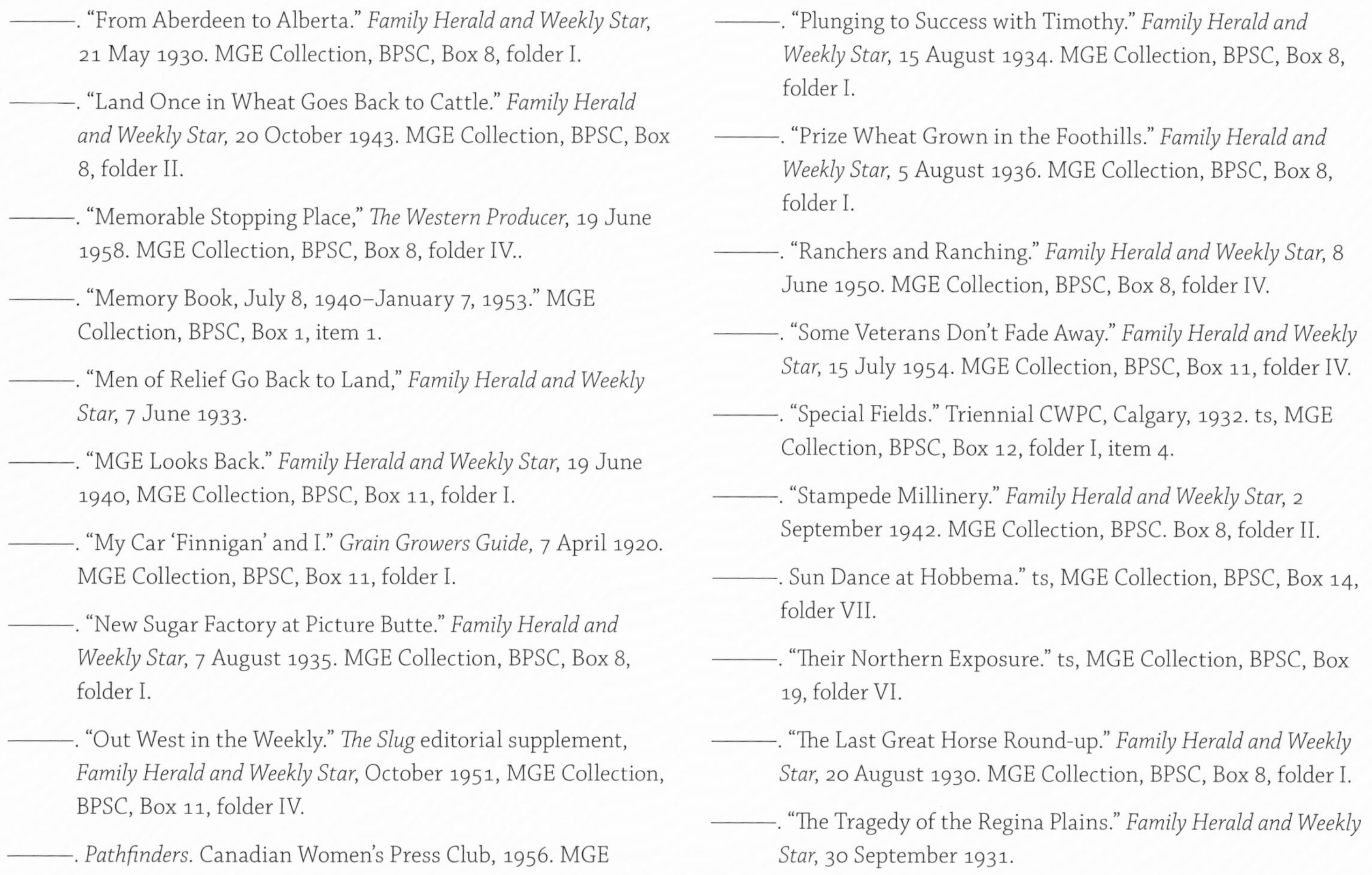

———. "From Aberdeen to Alberta." *Family Herald and Weekly Star,* 21 May 1930. MGE Collection, BPSC, Box 8, folder I.

———. "Land Once in Wheat Goes Back to Cattle." *Family Herald and Weekly Star,* 20 October 1943. MGE Collection, BPSC, Box 8, folder II.

———. "Memorable Stopping Place," *The Western Producer,* 19 June 1958. MGE Collection, BPSC, Box 8, folder IV..

———. "Memory Book, July 8, 1940–January 7, 1953." MGE Collection, BPSC, Box 1, item 1.

———. "Men of Relief Go Back to Land," *Family Herald and Weekly Star,* 7 June 1933.

———. "MGE Looks Back." *Family Herald and Weekly Star,* 19 June 1940, MGE Collection, BPSC, Box 11, folder I.

———. "My Car 'Finnigan' and I." *Grain Growers Guide,* 7 April 1920. MGE Collection, BPSC, Box 11, folder I.

———. "New Sugar Factory at Picture Butte." *Family Herald and Weekly Star,* 7 August 1935. MGE Collection, BPSC, Box 8, folder I.

———. "Out West in the Weekly." *The Slug* editorial supplement, *Family Herald and Weekly Star,* October 1951, MGE Collection, BPSC, Box 11, folder IV.

———. *Pathfinders.* Canadian Women's Press Club, 1956. MGE Collection, BPSC, Box 2, folder X. item 12.

———. "Plunging to Success with Timothy." *Family Herald and Weekly Star,* 15 August 1934. MGE Collection, BPSC, Box 8, folder I.

———. "Prize Wheat Grown in the Foothills." *Family Herald and Weekly Star,* 5 August 1936. MGE Collection, BPSC, Box 8, folder I.

———. "Ranchers and Ranching." *Family Herald and Weekly Star,* 8 June 1950. MGE Collection, BPSC, Box 8, folder IV.

———. "Some Veterans Don't Fade Away." *Family Herald and Weekly Star,* 15 July 1954. MGE Collection, BPSC, Box 11, folder IV.

———. "Special Fields." Triennial CWPC, Calgary, 1932. ts, MGE Collection, BPSC, Box 12, folder I, item 4.

———. "Stampede Millinery." *Family Herald and Weekly Star,* 2 September 1942. MGE Collection, BPSC. Box 8, folder II.

———. Sun Dance at Hobbema." ts, MGE Collection, BPSC, Box 14, folder VII.

———. "Their Northern Exposure." ts, MGE Collection, BPSC, Box 19, folder VI.

———. "The Last Great Horse Round-up." *Family Herald and Weekly Star,* 20 August 1930. MGE Collection, BPSC, Box 8, folder I.

———. "The Tragedy of the Regina Plains." *Family Herald and Weekly Star,* 30 September 1931.

———. *Travels and Tales of Miriam Green Ellis: Pioneer Journalist of the Canadian West*. Ed. Patricia Demers. Edmonton: University of Alberta Press, 2013.

———. "Watching Other People Farm." University Women's Club, Saskatoon, Saskatchewan. 15 January 1945 ts, MGE Collection, BPSC, Box 12, folder III, item 1.

———. "Western Homes I Have Seen." Manitoba Horticultural Association, 17 February 1943. ts, MGE Collection, BPSC, Box 12, folder II, item 7.

———. "The Women Grain Growers of Saskatchewan." *Woman's Century* March 1915, 11. *Feminism and the Periodical Press, 1900–1918*. Ed. Lucy Delap, Maria DiCenzo, and Leila Ryan. Vol 1. London: Routledge, 2006. 431.

———. "World's Best Wheat from Bush Land: Jack Caunck Returns from Chicago." *Family Herald and Weekly Star,* 18 December 1929. MGE Collection, BPSC, Box 8, folder I.

Fiamengo, Janice. *The Woman's Page; Journalism and Rhetoric in Early Canada*. Toronto: University of Toronto Press, 2008.

Gillilan, Strickland W. *Including Finnigin: A Book of Gillilan Verse*. Chicago: Forbes Company 1914.

Godsell, Jean W. *I Was No Lady: The Autobiography of a Fur Trader's Wife*. Toronto: Ryerson Press, 1959.

Haig, Kennethe Macmahon. *Brave Harvest: The Life Story of E. Cora Hind*. Toronto: Allen, 1945.

Hind, E. Cora. *My Travels and Findings*. Toronto: Macmillan Company of Canada, 1939.

———. *Seeing for Myself: Agricultural Conditions Around the World*. Toronto: Macmillan Company of Canada, 1937.

Jackel, Susan. "First Days, Fighting Days: Prairie Presswomen and Suffrage Activism, 1906–1916." *First Days, Fighting Days; Women in Manitoba History*. Ed. Mary Kinnear. Regina: Canadian Plains Research Center, University of Regina, 1987. 53–75.

"John D. Hunt is Honor Guest at Women's Press Club Soiree." *Edmonton Bulletin* 3 February 1919. Provincial Archives of Alberta Accession Number 74. 56 / 9.

LaFramboise, Lisa. "Miriam Green Ellis, 1881–1964." *The Small Details of Life; Twenty Diaries by Women in Canada*. Ed. Sarah Carter. Toronto: University of Toronto Press, 2002. 301–22.

Lang, Marjory. *Women Who Made the News: Female Journalists in Canada, 1880–1945*. Montreal and Kingston: McGill-Queen's University Press, 1999.

MacEwan, Grant. "Miriam Green Ellis: The Lady with the Notebook." *And Mighty Women Too: Stories of Notable Western Canadian Women*. Saskatoon, SK: Western Producer Prairie Books, 1975. 169–74.

MacLaren, I.S. and Lisa LaFramboise, editors. Introduction, *The Ladies, the Gwich'in, and the Rat*. Edmonton: University of Alberta Press, 1998. xv–xlix.

"Miriam Green Ellis." *Family Herald and Weekly Star*, 17 December 1964. MGE Collection, BPSC, Box 19, folder VI.

Oliver, Marjorie S. *Canadian Women's Press Club Golden Jubilee 1904–1954. Newspacket*. Toronto, 1954. Toronto Women's Press Club Archives, Doris Lewis Rare Book Room, University of Waterloo. GA 94, Accrual 1991, file 1.

Pettipas, Katherine. *Severing the Ties That Bind: Government Repression of Indigenous Religious Ceremonies on the Prairies*. Winnipeg: University of Manitoba Press, 1994.

Pratt, Mary Louise. *Imperial Eyes: Travel Writing and Transculturation*. Second edition. London: Routledge, 2008.

"Press Club Entertains in Honor of Miss Cora Hind." *Edmonton Journal* April 1919, n. pag. Provincial Archives of Alberta, Accession Number 74. 56 / 9.

Rex, Kay. *No Daughter of Mine: The Women and History of the Canadian Women's Press Club 1904–1971*. Toronto: Cedar Cave Books, 1995.

Scott, Joan Wallach. *The Fantasy of Feminist History*. Durham, NC: Duke University Press, 2011.

Steedman, Carolyn. *Dust: The Archive and Cultural History*. New Brunswick, NJ: Rutgers University Press, 2002.

Strong-Boag, Veronica. "Pulling in Double Harness or Hauling a Double Load: Women, Work and Feminism on the Canadian Prairie." *The Prairie West: Historical Readings*. Second ed. Ed. R. Douglas Francis and Howard Palmer. Edmonton: University of Alberta Press, 1992. 401–23.

"Sun Dance of the Crees at Hobbema: By Special Permission of Government Red Men Observe Wierd (*sic*) Ceremony." *Edmonton Journal* 21 July 1923, 3.

Taylor, Elizabeth R. "Up the Mackenzie River to the Polar Sea: A Lady's Journey in Arctic America" and "Articles Found Useful on My Mackenzie River Trip." *The Far Islands and Other Cold Places; Travel Essays of a Victorian Lady*. Ed. James Taylor Dunn. St. Paul, MN: Pogo Press, Inc., 1997. 50–62.

Textual Document Canadian Expeditionary Force Personnel, RG 150 Accession 1992/93 / 166 Box 2882-40. Record of Major George Ellis. Veterans Affairs section, Library and Archives Canada.

Vox Lycei: 1887–1937, Lisgar Collegiate Institute Year Book. Ed. John Fraser and Dick Barber. Ottawa: Lisgar Collegiate Institute, 1937.

Vyvyan, Clara. *Lady Vyvyan's Arctic Adventure. The Ladies, the Gwich'in, and the Rat; Travels on the Athabasca, Mackenzie, Rat, Porcupine, and Yukon Rivers in 1926*. Ed. I.S. MacLaren and Lisa LaFramboise. Edmonton: University of Alberta Press, 1998.

Wood, Louis Aubrey. *A History of Farmers' Movements in Canada: The Origins and Development of Agrarian Protest 1872–1924*. Toronto: University of Toronto Press, 1975.

Main body set in 12 pt Chaparral with a combination of FHA Condensed French, Rockwell, Typewriter MT, and BentonSans used for headings, footers, sidebars, and captions. Printed in four-colour process with an additional Pantone base colour on Cougar 100 lb. text and cover by McCallum Printing Group Inc., Edmonton, Alberta.

The variety of typefaces used in this design was chosen to portray different voices, from the main narrative and the tangential stories to the direct words of Miriam Green Ellis. Reminiscent of the wood type and slab serifs of the late 19th and early 20th centuries, and of the irregular text of the typewriter so well known to MGE, they bring together—in a playful juxtaposition—the vast experience of this adventurous woman.

Acknowledgements

All scholarship is a form of collaboration, especially so in this project, which is the result of partnerships and generous academic exchange. In the first instance I want to thank Robert Desmarais, Head of the Bruce Peel Special Collections Library, for inviting me to prepare this exhibit. A few years ago, Special Collections librarian Jeannine Green actually introduced me to MGE, half-suspecting how easily hooked I would become. Working with always-accommodating colleagues in the Peel Library, Robert, Carol Irwin, Jeff Papineau, and Linda Quirk, has been a genuine pleasure. The ease with which they have anticipated my many requests has been invaluable, and the thoughtful care with which Carol and Jeff have arranged the exhibit and its accompanying attractions, along with the expert photography of MGE's material objects by Michael Chevalier, has been so very gratifying. Designer Lara Minja has translated our shared excitement about MGE into this beautiful catalogue, astutely edited by Leslie Vermeer. The Peel Library's partnership with the University of Alberta Press to launch *Travels and Tales of Miriam Green Ellis: Pioneer Journalist of the Canadian West* (print, epub, and kindle) in conjunction with this catalogue, mounted exhibit, and online exhibit illustrates how established and innovative technology can support and enhance one another. I am deeply grateful to colleagues at the Press, director Linda Cameron, editors Peter Midgley and Mary Lou Roy, designer Alan Brownoff, and marketing manager Cathie Crooks, who have made collaboration a sheer pleasure. Mille mercis!

Left: Manœuvring the Rapids [magic lantern slide] 96-91 MGE S1
Right: "Horse stuck crossing Salt River" [magic lantern slide] 96-91 MGE S1